Praise for Lori Duron's *Raising My Rainbow*

"Lori Duron, a writer of extraordinary generosity, has given us a guide to parenthood both gentle and revolutionary. *Raising My Rainbow* is a valuable resource not only for parents of gender-nonconforming children, but for readers everywhere who seek the courage to stand up for the ones they love. Fierce, wise, and illuminating."

—Jennifer Finney Boylan, author of *She's Not There* and *Stuck in the Middle with You*

"Because of Lori's courage, there is now an answer when searching for how to parent a child who is gender fluid, gender nonconforming, transgender, gay, or whatever label you use. This book is a wonderfully authentic read that will bring depth, joy, and understanding to parents, extended families, and anyone seeking to learn how parents can and do love gender-creative children. To acceptance!"

—Cheryl Kilodavis, author of *My Princess Boy*

"[A]n optimistic and delightful memoir . . . Duron's call for compassion should be heeded by educators, caregivers, and neighbors—an open heart, a desire to listen and learn, and a willingness to accommodate go a long way in doing well by someone who differs from your expectations."

—*Publishers Weekly,* starred review

"A powerful book at the right time."

—Andy Cohen, author of *Most Talkative*

"It takes a village to raise a child, and it takes a gender-creative parent to create a gender-creative child. Lori Duron is just one of those parents, and *Raising My Rainbow* is a must-read for the entire village. Beautifully written, humorous, and deeply open and self-reflective, this book, the first of its kind, gives us a window into a mother's joys, pain, and courage raising a child who goes against the binary gender grain of our society. This is not only an outstanding book, it is a big step forward in making it a better world for all of us."

—Diane Ehrensaft, author of *Gender Born, Gender Made*

"First drawn to Lori's work as an educator and LGBT activist, it was my role as a father that provided the most poignant critical lens for *Raising My Rainbow*. While nobody has a blueprint for parenting, Lori's compassionate, insightful, and yes, humorous take on raising a gender creative child should be required reading for anyone bringing up or working with children."

—Frank Bua, author of *Lost and Found,* and board member, Family Equality Council

"I fell in love with this. Lori Duron has written a very important book, and as an author she is extremely generous in sharing the story of her family and in particular her own journey which made her realize that her job regarding her son is to 'not change him but to love him.' Duron and her husband and older son beautifully rise to every challenge C.J.'s gender creativity presents to them. As a reader, I felt privileged to witness their journey."

—Lesléa Newman, author of *The Boy Who Cried Fabulous, Heather Has Two Mommies,* and *October Mourning*

"Lori Duron has painted an exquisite picture of the complex journey that is raising a gender-diverse child. In chronicling her family's transformation from confusion to fear, to acceptance, and ultimately to fierce pride, she has provided an unwavering celebration of her child's gender self-determination. Not just a book for families with gender-nonconforming children, *Raising My Rainbow* is a wonderful resource for all parents committed to honoring children for who they are."

—Joel Baum, director of Education and Training, Gender Spectrum

"Laugh-out-loud funny, tug-at-the-heartstrings moving, and thoroughly thought provoking, *Raising My Rainbow* is a must-read for anyone who has ever worried that their child—or a child that they know—might be perceived as 'different from' or 'other than.'"

—Jody M. Huckaby, executive director of PFLAG National

RAISING MY RAINBOW

Adventures in Raising a

Fabulous, Gender Creative Son

LORI DURON

B \ D \ W \ Y
BROADWAY BOOKS
NEW YORK

Copyright © 2013 by Lori Duron

Published in the United States by Broadway Books, an imprint of the
Crown Publishing Group, a division of Random House, Inc., New York.
www.crownpublishing.com

BROADWAY BOOKS and its logo, B\D\W\Y,
are trademarks of Random House, Inc.

Library of Congress Cataloging-in-Publication Data
Duron, Lori.
Raising my rainbow : adventures in raising a fabulous, gender creative son /
Lori Duron.
1. Parents of gays. 2. Child rearing. 3. Child psychology. I. Title.
HQ759.9145 .D87 2013
306.874—dc23   2012042444

ISBN 978-0-7704-3772-5
eISBN 978-0-7704-3771-8

PRINTED IN THE UNITED STATES OF AMERICA

Book design by Elizabeth Rendfleisch
Cover design by Lynn Buckley
Cover photograph: Mike Flippo
Author photograph: Rebecca Dever

3 5 7 9 10 8 6 4

First Edition

For Matt

And for C.M., C.J., and M.L.

Foreword

By David Burtka and Neil Patrick Harris

We first found out about *Raising My Rainbow* while discussing our twins and their development with some friends. It was the type of conversation that new parents have all the time. Mostly, these discussions revolve around retelling stories of our toddlers' silly antics, showing off their latest and very nuanced finger-painting accomplishments (we can't help but be proud), or if we're really lucky, unveiling some new development in stroller-folding technology that is guaranteed to free up more trunk space for our double diaper bags. Why are strollers so big?

But, in truth, we scour these seemingly breezy conversations for any sign of parenting expertise we may have missed. It's our way of soothing the nagging fear that some critical information on child rearing has been overlooked, despite our reading a myriad of books on child raising, scrolling the Internet for product recalls till 2:00 a.m., grilling our parents for the "wisdom of the ages," and seeking the advice of doctors at the slightest sniffle. Like many, we are parents who want answers for everything.

So, we began reading the *Raising My Rainbow* blog. Mostly

out of curiosity at first. After all, neither of our children had demonstrated any signs of wanting to push gender boundaries. In fact, quite the opposite was true. Harper loves dresses and hairstyles. Gideon wants to take everything apart to see how it works. Our kids seemed comfortable in this regard and, except that none of Gideon's cars have wheels on them, we were too. So, we decided to accept our living room as a miniature auto body shop and moved on.

But we kept reading the blog (and later the book you're sure to pick up and won't be able to put down). We were struck by the stories about C.J. As far as we know, *Raising My Rainbow* is the first book published by a parent of a gender nonconforming child. We became enthralled by the challenges he and his parents face, which are so different than ours. We admired their bravery for striking out into uncharted territory and wondered if maybe it was the bravery of little C.J. that gives them that strength. After all, there's something inherently powerful and beautiful about a child's natural unobstructed instincts for play and creativity. We see it in our own children every day. But it also takes a lot of consideration to know how to best balance a child's instincts with the need to guide and protect them. It's our role as parents. We were fascinated with the daring balance C.J.'s family chose to strike and empathized with their fear of not knowing what the outcome of their parenting choices would be.

But, beyond being fascinated with this family and awed by their level of communication and trust, that nagging blip was still there on our baby radar, searching for that missing kernel of knowledge. . . . What was the takeaway for us?

Then it hit us. Despite how unique this book's story is, in it we found a commonality that all families share. We all want what's best for our children. We are all desperate to make the right decisions for them, often in the face of a lot of very serious unknowns. We may not all agree with each other's choices, but in the end, we share one thing: we would give anything, absolutely anything, to see them grow up happy and healthy.

Parenting is a scary place to be, for all of us. No matter what scope of challenges our little bundles of joy present. It's certainly the biggest, most challenging role we've ever taken on. And one we're so glad to not have to take on alone.

Thanks C.J.

Chapter 1

MY FIVE-YEAR-OLD SON, C.J., is ready for school. He's wearing his favorite pink-and-white striped polo shirt and khaki shorts. His teeth are brushed and so is his short auburn hair. He's standing in front of the full-length mirror in my bedroom, where he feels close to me, as I get dressed for work. I brush my brown hair, create a side part, and pull it back into a low ponytail. He pretend-braids his imaginary long blonde hair and ties a bow at the end. I slip on silver hoop earrings and fasten them. He pretends to do the same. I zip up the back of my dress as he slides on a few revolutions of imaginary lipstick. I put on my black high heels and he straightens his imaginary tiara. I give myself a spritz of perfume as he arrives beside me and puffs out his chest. I give him a pretend spray or two. I grab my computer bag, he grabs his Monster High lunch box, and we head out the door—he to kindergarten and I to the office.

As we part ways for the day, I say to him, "I love you no matter what." It's the absolute truth. There are no conditions or expectations. I love him no matter what.

Hours later, I load my smiling son into the car. As I drive

home, he pulls papers out of his folder to show me. He holds up a worksheet on which he has been practicing writing the letter *B*. "B is for Bear," the worksheet says. C.J. colored his bear pink and purple with long blonde hair, hoop earrings, red lipstick, and long pink fingernails.

"Look, Mommy, my bear's fingernails match my finger-nails!" he squeals in giddy delight, kicking his feet, which dangle down from his booster seat, his pink polka-dot Minnie Mouse socks peeking out from his mint green tennis shoes.

"They sure do," I say as I stop at a traffic light and turn to smile at my special boy. His pink glitter fingernails sparkle in the sun as he holds them next to his bear's fingernails for me to compare and admire.

"I picked the color special. My teacher said we could color the bear any colors we wanted. I made sure I asked. I didn't want to color mine brown like real bears. Brown is boring," he says. I will learn later that all of the other kids colored their bears traditional colors like white, brown, and black. My son has always shied away from the traditional, the "boring."

When we get home, C.J. dashes up the stairs to his Monster High–themed bedroom to change out of his school clothes and into his pink Hello Kitty skirt and white lace tank top. Every day I can almost hear and feel him exhale when he changes out of his "school clothes" and into his "dress-up clothes." It's as if, for the first time all day, he is truly comfortable. He clips on his pink rhinestone butterfly earrings and, as he flits down the stairs holding a Barbie doll, I catch a glimpse of his Superman boxer briefs.

As I cook dinner, he helps himself to a fresh piece of white paper and sketches what looks like a girl with long red hair, full pink lips in the shape of a puffy heart, a blue dress, rainbow tights, red shoes, a purple tiara, hazel green eyes, and a dozen freckles that rest on the bridge of her feminine nose. I don't have to ask who the girl in the picture is; I know that it is my son. I'd recognize him anywhere.

C.J. is gender nonconforming, gender creative, gender fluid, gender independent, gender variant, has gender identity disorder, or whatever you prefer to call it. For more than half of his life, my son hasn't conformed to traditional gender norms. As C.J. explains it, he's "a boy who likes girl stuff and wants to be treated like a girl."

My firstborn son, Chase, arrives home from flag football practice, bounding through the door, dropping his backpack in the middle of the kitchen floor as he moves toward the fridge for a snack. As I tell him that dinner is almost ready and snacking is not an option, I kiss the top of his head. He is sweaty and smells like elementary school and pigskin practice—a mix of playground, lunch, number-two pencils, leather, and wet grass.

Chase is all boy and always has been. He's like his dad in that respect. My husband, Matt, is my high-school sweetheart and has been for more than eighteen years. He's an Irishman with a heart of gold hidden underneath his tough-guy facade and ever-present scowl. He has delicious strawberry blonde hair, light blue eyes, and broad, strong shoulders. He's a guy's guy with a motorcycle, oversized truck, classic car, pool table, dartboard, and kegerator.

Matt and I thought, when we had a second boy, that we

would just get more of the same, that when Chase finished a particular phase or stage, C.J. would enter it and we'd do it all over again. We thought wrong.

We thought that our two boys might have slightly different interests. One might like baseball more, while the other preferred soccer. One might like LEGOs, while the other preferred Hot Wheels. We anticipated that their taste in "boy things" might differ slightly. What we didn't anticipate was that one of our boys might like "girl toys," "girl clothes," and hanging out with girls in general. We never, in a million years, thought that we would have a boy who was a girl at heart.

On the gender-variation spectrum of super-macho-masculine on the left all the way to super-girly-feminine on the right, C.J. slides fluidly in the middle; he's neither all pink nor all blue. He's a muddled mess or a rainbow creation, depending on how you look at it. Matt and I have decided to see the rainbow, not the muddle. But we didn't always see it that way.

Initially, the sight of our son playing with girl toys or wearing girl clothes made our chests tighten, forged a lump in our throats, and, at times, made us want to hide him. There was anger, anxiety, and fear. We've evolved as parents as our younger son has evolved into a fascinating, vibrant person who is creative with gender. Sometimes, when I think of how we behaved as parents early in C.J.'s gender nonconformity, I'm ashamed and embarrassed.

Chapter 2

IT WAS LIKE WATCHING SOMEBODY come alive, watching a flower bloom, watching a rainbow cross the sky. It was the day that C.J. discovered Barbie. He was two and a half years old.

One late fall afternoon, as I was doing some cleaning, I found a boxed Barbie in the depths of my closet and tossed her on my bed.

"WHAT DAT?!"

I wobbled and nearly fell off my stepladder at C.J.'s shriek.

"It's Barbie," I said, regaining my balance.

This particular Barbie was pretty fabulous. It was Mattel's 50th Anniversary Bathing Suit Barbie. She was a modernized version of the original 1959 doll, with a two-piece, black-and-white bikini trimmed with her signature color pink; pink hoop earrings; a long blonde ponytail; and a pink cell phone.

"I want to open she!" C.J. declared.

He held the box as he jumped up and down, up and down, up and down. I'm sure he gave Barbie a concussion. I hesitated. I had been trained well by my mother; you don't open a boxed Barbie if you can at all help it. I was a little annoyed; I was going to open the box and take Barbie out, and my son was going to play with her for a few seconds and move on to something else bright and shiny. Then I'd be left with a depreciated piece of plastic. But his face, his sweet excited face could convince me to do worse things. We opened her.

In that instant, our lives changed forever in a way that we never expected. In our family's history there is now B.B. (Before Barbie) and A.B. (After Barbie). Never underestimate the power of an eleven-and-a-half-inch woman.

Of course, at that exact moment, I wasn't aware that our lives were changing. I couldn't have predicted the magnitude of C.J.'s actions or mine. I figured that C.J. would play with Barbie for a day, maybe two, and lose interest—as he had with all of the other toys he had encountered in his short life. I was wrong; Barbie has been a constant in his life since that day. Oh, my son wasn't dabbling; he was hard-core from the start. C.J. had found his life's passion—and he wasn't even three.

Matt arrived home from work at the police department to spy a big-busted blonde in his younger son's grip. He shot me a look that said, *What the hell is that?* I replied with a glance that whispered, *Settle down. We'll talk about it later.*

Matt changed out of his uniform and sat on the living room floor next to C.J., who was sitting criss-cross-applesauce and trying his hardest to put clothes back on a naked Barbie.

"What do you got there, buddy?" Matt asked C.J.

C.J.'s eyes lit up and a huge grin crossed his face as he excitedly described the doll in great detail to his father. I smiled from my spot at the kitchen sink.

Later that night, after C.J. and Chase were asleep, Matt shared with me the unease he'd felt when he saw his son playing with a doll. Having grown up with no sisters, he'd never even had a Barbie in his house before and couldn't remember ever touching one. It didn't feel right to him, though it didn't feel completely wrong either. After all, C.J. was just a child and Barbie was just a toy.

It was the first of thousands of conversations we've had in the privacy of our bedroom late at night as we've tried to figure out how best to parent a boy who, at times, is clearly more girl.

"My brother played with Barbies," I reasoned with Matt, reminding myself and trying to squash the indescribable feelings of unease we were flirting with. "And he turned out fine."

Matt gave me a look that expanded on my last sentence. *Fine and gay.*

Of course C.J.'s zeal for Barbie reminded me of my brother, Michael.

My brother and I had a bad Barbie habit as kids. While other kids we knew were committed to karate, baseball, piano, and dance, we were committed to playing with Barbies. We did it all the time, just as I assumed all brothers and sisters did. I didn't realize until much later in life that my family's definition of "normal" was different from other families'.

On any given weekend Michael and I would convert the entire floor of the front family room into a fabulous world for our Barbies. There was a wardrobe area and a styling area for accessories, hair, and makeup. We arranged the miniature furniture to create a spacious four-bedroom, one-story, ranch-style home, since we weren't fortunate enough to possess the Dream House or even the Malibu Beach House. We convinced ourselves that ours was way better anyway, because it was custom-built, our lot size was bigger, and we could keep our brown plastic horse in our backyard.

Sometimes we'd create a mall, and our Barbies, Kens, Skippers, and Midges would all go shopping and eat in the food court, where some one-off Barbie who had suffered some sort of disfigurement (such as a bad haircut, a lost limb, or general disrepair) would take their order and serve them lunch from Hot Dog on a Stick.

I called my brother.

"Guess what C.J. found when I was cleaning out my closet?" I asked.

"Your vibrator?"

"No, you idiot, he found one of my Barbies."

"You still have Barbies?! How come you never get them out when I come over?" he said, his feelings genuinely hurt, as if I sat my thirtysomething-year-old ass around playing Barbies all day every day and then hid them when he visited.

"It's one Barbie. Mom just gave it to me. It's the fiftieth-anniversary Barbie," I said, trying to get to the point.

"How come she didn't get me one? This is just like when we were kids; you always got the Barbies and I didn't. I got footballs. I hate footballs."

"This isn't about you. C.J. found the Barbie and *loves* her. He's obsessed," I explained.

"Oh," my brother said quietly. "What do you think it means?"

"I don't know," I said, although I knew exactly what I thought it meant: my two-and-a-half-year-old son was gay.

Chapter 3

FOR DAYS AFTER C.J. discovered her, Barbie never left his side. When I'd do a final bed check at night before I retired for the evening to watch reality television and sneak chocolate when no one was looking, I'd see his full head of auburn hair sticking out above his covers. Next to him there would be a tiny tuft of blonde hair sticking out as well.

The next time we were at Target and near the toy aisle—which I've always tried to pass at warp speed so the kids don't notice and beg me to buy them something—C.J. wanted to see "Barbie stuff." I led him to the appropriate aisle and he stood there transfixed, not touching a thing, just taking it all in. He was so overwhelmed that he didn't ask to buy a single thing. He finally walked away from the aisle speechless, as if he had just seen something so magical and majestic that he needed time to process it.

He had, that day, discovered the pink aisles of the toy department. We had never been down those aisles; we had only frequented the blue aisles, when we ventured down the toy aisles at all. As far as C.J. was concerned, I had been hiding half of the world from him.

I felt bad about that, like I had deprived him because of my assumptions and expectations that he was a boy and boys liked boy things. Matt and I had noticed that C.J. didn't really like any of the toys we provided for him, which were all handed down from his brother. We noticed that C.J. didn't go through the normal boy toy addictions that Chase had gone through: he couldn't care less about balls, cars, dinosaurs, superheroes, The Wiggles, Bob the Builder, or Thomas the Tank Engine. What did he like to play with? We didn't worry ourselves much about finding the answer (a case of the second-born child not getting fussed over quite like the firstborn); we trusted that in time something would draw him in. Which it did. It just wasn't at all what we were expecting.

At about the eighteen- to twenty-four-month mark of a child's life, the gender-neutral toys disappear and toys that are marketed specifically to boys or to girls take over. We didn't realize it until later, but that divide in the toy world and our house being filled with only boy toys left C.J. a little lost at playtime. We and the rest of society had been pushing masculine stuff on him and enforcing traditional gender norms, when all he wanted was to brush long blonde hair and dress, undress, and re-dress Barbie, occasionally rubbing her boobs for comfort as some rub a rabbit's foot for good luck.

I should have known better, I really should have. I grew up with a boy who preferred girl toys and girl things to boy stuff. When I was really young, I didn't question it because the great gender divide hadn't been introduced to me; I was uncorrupted by contrived notions of how kids should play and what they should play with based on the sex box checked on their birth certificate. When I got older and became aware of the amount of time my brother actually spent playing with girl toys and doing girl things, I figured that he only did them with me and only to make me happy because he was the best big brother a girl could ask for. I surmised that he was doing me a favor when, in reality, I was doing him a favor. I was his excuse to act out his every effeminate whim. My brother was gender nonconforming at heart at a time and in a place where it wasn't discussed, let alone embraced.

When my brother was a child, our mother indulged his feminine fancies here and there and tried to help him conform when she felt that it was in his best interest, which was often. Bless her heart; she was a teen mom doing the best she could.

My mother has always been a lady. She swears that she was a tomboy as a child, but I have a hard time believing her. She takes two hours to get ready every morning and has been like that my entire life. Growing up, we were late to every event to which we were invited, but don't you know that when we did arrive, her hair was set and sprayed, her pantyhose were just the right shade of nude, and her outfit was perfectly pressed. For all of my childhood she smelled of White Shoulders.

She's the most patient person I've met in my life and optimistic as hell. She doesn't speak sarcasm or witty humor— which is weird because it is the native language of her two offspring. There's an innate need in her to please people.

When she met and married my father, a lot of things changed. The two of them and a three-year-old Michael started making a life together. My father started pointing out the things Michael did that weren't exactly masculine. He would know; he was the oldest of five boys.

My father is a devout born-again Christian and macho Mexican American who doesn't seem to care much for weakness in men or fearlessness in women. I always knew that he loved my brother and me. I can't say that my brother always felt that love, but my father provided for our family and filled the father role that my brother's biological father had given up without a fight. He tried to help my brother become the kind of man that he himself was, when that wasn't at all what my brother wanted—because he was busy wishing he could be more like my mother and me.

In me, Michael saw a person whom he could love no matter what and who would love him unconditionally. Fortunately for him, I fulfilled that vision. He's confided in me that he doesn't know what he would have done if I hadn't been born. At the time of my birth he was nine years old and felt stifled, as if he had to hide his true self. He felt shame because he was a sissy.

I always felt lucky that I was a girl and was able to do all of the girly things that my brother wanted to do but couldn't because he was a boy. But I felt like a tomboy, too. I wanted to play with the boy toys my brother had, wear his hand-me-downs, and pee standing up. I wanted to be just like him, which to me meant being part boy and part girl. I'd play with his Star Wars action figures while wearing an Incredible Hulk shirt, then play dress-up in my mother's nightgowns and pretend to breastfeed my Cabbage Patch Kid dolls.

I had never focused so much on the details of our childhood, I'd never spent so much time ruminating about my brother's gender expression, his eventual sexuality, and the effect my mother and father's parenting had on our lives, until C.J. picked up that Barbie. How could it be? How could our family have *another* boy who liked everything about being a girl? What were the chances?

Chapter 4

"HOW LONG DO YOU REALLY think this phase is going to last?" Matt asked me one evening a few weeks after Barbie, as C.J. was in his room playing with Barbie and Chase was in his room building with LEGOs.

"I don't know—Chase was into Thomas the Tank Engine from exactly his third birthday to exactly his fourth birthday, so twelve months, I guess," I responded, like I had it all figured out and wasn't confused by the feelings I had over my son playing with Barbie. "I wouldn't expect for it to go on longer than that; that was a pretty intense phase by kid standards."

I had been keeping myself busy by thinking about expected time frames, all while knowing, deep down, that C.J. wasn't going to tire of Barbie anytime soon. There was an audio loop in my uneasy head that was on repeat. *Settle down. . . . It's just a phase. . . . It doesn't mean anything. . . . This too shall pass. . . . He's only two. . . . It's only one Barbie.*

I couldn't catalog my emotions or thoughts. It was cute seeing my son playing with a doll and being so enamored with something for the first time in his life. But there were moments when it felt unnatural and a little jarring. Sometimes it was frustrating. I had always thought of myself as a liberal, nonjudgmental, and progressive person, but obviously I wasn't, or feelings of unease would never have flitted through my head.

More often than not, I felt like I needed to offer an explanation about my son's behaviors and preferences, even when nobody asked for one. I wanted to have reasons why he gravitated toward anything considered feminine, why he was fascinated by the way fabric and hair moved, and why he preferred the company of females to that of males. But I had no explanation. I couldn't explain my child. That was the worst feeling of all.

There were also intensely happy mommy moments as I watched my child absorbed in play with Barbie, because that was when he was truly happiest. That's when the smile on his face beamed the brightest. That's when all seemed right in his world. How could playing with dolls and gender roles be wrong when it looked like it felt so right?

Christmas that year came at a very odd time. C.J. had found Barbie three months earlier and was showing a preference for girl toys whenever there was an option, but Matt and I weren't sure how to move forward. Did C.J. like girl toys because they were a novelty? Would he like boy toys if those were all he had? What were we supposed to do? Encourage this untraditional behavior or help him conform to stereotypes that the rest of society expected? We tried to walk a fine line.

On Christmas morning C.J. rushed down the stairs to the tree to find his presents, and all of his unbridled excitement quickly turned into lackluster contentment. He received a few gender-neutral puzzles, some arts-and-crafts supplies, books, a blue baby stroller, a baby doll dressed in all blue, and a plain white car for his Barbie to ride in. A stroller and baby doll are typically considered girls' toys, but in all blue they felt like they could still safely be appropriate for a boy. The sweet ride we got for Barbie was, obviously, from the girls' section of the toy department but was, after all, a car, so it was still technically a boy toy. My overthinking C.J.'s gifts left us missing the mark completely. He was less than thrilled with his new toys, and the feelings of disappointment that wafted from him as bedtime approached made me want to remove all of the Christmas decorations and forget about the holiday altogether. I should have bought him another damn Barbie.

Matt and I went to bed Christmas night feeling horrible, as if we had cheated our kid. Chase had fallen asleep exhausted, with a smile on his face, surrounded by new toys he loved. C.J. lay in bed talking gibberish to his one Barbie, like every other night. His brand-new toys were in the corner of his room being ignored.

"Well, we really screwed that one up," Matt said.

"I know, but it's so hard to know what to do. He's never really liked any toys, and we don't know if this is just a phase. And I mean, will anything compare to that first Barbie at this point?" I said.

Silence.

"We got him girl toys!" I argued.

Matt looked at me.

"Kind of," I said.

"Barely," he said. "Next year we're not doing that."

I nodded my head in agreement. Hopefully next year we'd have our son all figured out. Now I can look back and know that it was our feelings—not our son—that needed to be figured out.

Because she was the only girl toy he owned and, therefore, the only toy C.J. would play with, that first Barbie got absolutely thrashed. She slept with C.J., ate with C.J., lay on the wet bathroom counter and brushed teeth with C.J., bathed with C.J., and fell down our stairs multiple times when C.J. lost his otherwise firm hold on her. She had her hair braided, unbraided, and rebraided. She had it severely tangled several times and had a run-in with a peanut-butter-and-jelly sandwich that did not end in her favor. She had ponytails and pigtails and something that looked like a rabbit's tail. She lost her shorts and couldn't call someone for a new pair because she lost her cell phone, too.

In January, with C.J.'s third birthday only one month away, it was time for potty training. In our family we use the industry-standard method to get the number ones and twos in the bowl and out of the pants: bribery. If he got a turd in the toilet, we would take him to Target and he could pick out any toy he wanted.

"Even a girl toy?!" he asked.

Even a girl toy.

Mere hours later we heard one of the most glorious sounds in the world. Something of substance hit toilet water. C.J. had pooped in the potty. Chase was the first one to cheer. He had been sitting on a step stool in the bathroom keeping C.J. company while he tried to master potty training. Chase would read books to C.J., and they would sing songs and tell each other jokes. It was cute to watch, and since it kept them both busy, you can imagine how nice it was for me.

I wiped C.J. and we were out of there. We entered Target and the boys literally ran full speed to the pink aisles of the toy section. When I found them there, C.J. was holding a box containing Disney's Belle from *Beauty and the Beast*. She was Barbie-sized, in a lavish gold gown and wearing a necklace with a rose pendant. When C.J. pushed the rose, Belle sang. He smiled. I took his picture right then and there, holding the box and grinning an award-winning grin. He was freshly pooped and happy in the pink aisles of a megaretailer, holding a doll he had obviously been coveting. We were in celebration mode and I didn't care who saw us.

I texted Matt, who was at work, a photo of C.J.'s crap in the toilet and the picture of him holding Belle at Target.

"WAY TO GO, BUDDY!" Matt texted back for me to read to C.J.

I posted the photo of C.J. and Belle to Facebook (which is the closest thing to a baby book C.J. will ever have) with a caption that read, "C.J. pooped in the potty for the first time and he got to pick out any toy he wanted." I was one proud mama.

"Are you serious? He wanted a doll?" a male Facebook friend commented on the photo instantly.

Yes. Ugh, my Facebook friend's questions annoyed me, but I wasn't going to let it get to me. Not on a day of victory; I'd unfriend him later.

C.J. carried Belle proudly all the way to the checkout counter, where he gently laid her on the conveyer belt. She slid slowly to the cashier under his watchful eye.

"My brother pooped in the potty. That's why he's getting a toy," Chase announced, putting his arm around C.J. proudly.

"Good job!" the cashier said.

"I pooped in the potty today too, but I guess I don't get a toy," Chase said, looking at me.

C.J.'s collection of girl toys basically doubled with the purchase of Belle. Rather quickly he threw Strawberry Shortcake, Zoobles, Littlest Pet Shop, and Squinkies into the mix, thanks to my mother, whom my children call Nana.

We also call her Nana Grab Bags because she carries an oversized T.J.Maxx purse filled with candy, toys, hugs, and zany theories from which she grabs freely and dispenses without regard to pretty much anything.

Nothing in her world compares to Chase and C.J. Her love for them is beyond unconditional and she grants their wishes without thought. Perhaps not surprisingly, this has caused some of our biggest mother-daughter fights.

We had asked her not to buy C.J. girl stuff without our permission. We were trying to figure out what was going on with our son and how we were feeling. We thought that maybe if he didn't have girl stuff he wouldn't like girl stuff. But Nana bought it for him anyway.

"Why won't you listen to us?" I asked my mother one day when I picked up C.J. from her house and he was playing with a new Polly Pocket doll she had bought for him.

"I just can't resist him. He wanted it so badly, and you should have seen his little face," she said.

I sat there quietly with thoughts running rampant in my head and making no sense. It was as if there were static on my brain's screen accompanied by white noise and I couldn't change the channel or get better reception.

"What are you so afraid of?" my mother asked me quietly and in a way that only a mother can.

Naturally, I teared up. The answer came to me, finally, clear as high definition.

"I'm afraid that he'll get teased. That we'll get teased. I'm afraid of what other people will think and say."

I had said it. It was my gut response that had been buried and unexplainable, hiding for the last four months, until that moment. It felt like a relief to pinpoint my feelings and concerns and to say them out loud. Then it pissed me off royally, because I have never been one to care what other people think. I had identified my biggest fear in raising a child like C.J., but I wasn't ready to conquer that fear and set it free. It would be months and months before I learned to do that.

Initially, we set rules and compromises that I am now ashamed to admit. All girl toys had to stay at home; they couldn't leave the house when we did, under the ruse that we didn't want to lose them. Barbie was our little secret. Eventually the girl toys could come with us but had to stay in the car because we "didn't want them to get lost or dirty." Then they could go in certain places that felt safe to Matt and me. The grocery store was okay because everybody was busy doing their own thing. Chase's school was not okay, because Chase might get teased because of his brother's preference in toys. C.J. was confused by our parenting tactics and all of the rules he had to take into consideration before leaving the house. He couldn't keep it all straight—and neither could we. He started to question us, trying to persuade us and sneaking his "girl things" into places when he thought we weren't looking. All of life had become an exhausting, hypervigilant negotiation.

Chapter 5

WHILE WE TRIED TO SET BOUNDARIES, C.J.'s love of all things pink, purple, sparkly, glittery, and frilly knew no bounds. I realized the gravity of our plight when not only could C.J. name each Disney Princess and her movie of origin, but so could Matt and Chase. C.J. had grown to love the Disney Princesses so much that when his third birthday finally rolled around, he wanted a Disney Princess–themed party.

Where we live, in conservative and competitive Orange County, California, third birthdays are when things start to get out of control. It happens right around the time there are preschool classmates and parents to impress. In Orange County—especially the southernmost portion, where we live, where you can run into a Real Housewife in the grocery store or at the gym—people are constantly trying to one-up and outdo one another. Kids' birthday parties are a big deal here. There are mobile salons that cater to tweens and mobile video-game trucks that bring every gaming system and every video game to your driveway so that the pint-sized party peeps can get their game on in an air-conditioned fifth wheel. We've been to kids' parties that were fully catered and have left with goody bags that cost more than the gift we brought. (To some that may say more about us than about the party's host. I get it.) It's an unspoken rule that you'll invite every classmate, because you wouldn't want to hurt anybody's feelings. Each classmate is accompanied by at least one parent, and sometimes a sibling or two is in tow, throwing the group dynamic even more off kilter.

C.J. had been to enough of these over-the-top parties to know that he wanted one for himself, with as many people in attendance as possible and with the house and his cake decked out with Disney Princesses. There was no room for negotiation.

It was the first but definitely not the last time I thought, *Great, my son is going to be the punch line of some gay joke.*

I worried that some partygoer would take a photo of the birthday boy blowing out pink glitter candles atop a Disney Princess–themed cake and post that photo on Facebook with some slightly homophobic, sassy caption and that that person's Facebook friends would try to outwit one another with LGBTQ-unfriendly, snarky comments. Obviously I'm good at brainstorming worst-case scenarios.

Finally, the big day came, and it was almost time to sing "Happy Birthday." Friends and family were gathered around the table outside by the pool. So were the preschool classmates and their parents, all strangers to us.

Nana Grab Bags exited the kitchen and approached the crowd first. She proudly carried a tray of homemade gender-neutral-yellow cupcakes that had been rainbow-sprinkled to perfection. In her blue maxidress she moved like Cinderella's godmother.

I was right behind her carrying C.J.'s oversized cupcake adorned with Ariel, Belle, Aurora, Cinderella, Snow White, even Jasmine.

Nana Grab Bags set the cupcakes in the center of the table. All eyes were on us.

I set the jumbo pink princess cupcake with pastel sprinkles in front of C.J. as everyone watched. C.J. was clapping his hands out of excitement and in approval of his cake. His smile was wide and his dimples were deep. It was the cake of his dreams.

The group turned into a mixture of skeptical looks, baffled expressions, and smirky smiles. No one said a word to us. People were using their smartphones to capture the moment. More so than usual—or at least that's how it felt. It seemed like every partygoer wanted a shot of the birthday boy with his princess cake. I held my head up high and carried on, as if this were perfectly normal, because, increasingly, for us, it was.

It felt like a coming-out party for our family, like we were saying to everyone in attendance, *This is our son, he is three, and he likes girl stuff. If you don't like it, you can take your goody bag and go.* It was nerve-racking for us, but we tried to remember that the day was about C.J., not us or anybody else. When it was over, we breathed a sigh of relief, wondered if there would be any fallout, and dreaded seeing the other parents at school on Monday.

"What did we do for C.J.'s first birthday? I can't remember," Matt said when we had cleaned up the party mess and restored our house to its usual happy, messy order.

"Remember, I went to Party City got all of the 'baby boy's

first birthday' decorations they had, and we had a blue-teddy-bear theme, and Nana Grab Bags made the sweetest little teddy-bear cake, and I practically covered the entire house in baby blue," I said, reminiscing and smiling at the picture in my head of C.J. wearing cake on his face and a blue birthday hat on his head.

"Oh, yeah. C.J. probably hated it with all that blue. Poor guy."

My smile evaporated. I wanted to get defensive because it felt like an affront, since I had been the party planner. How was I supposed to know—before he could really express himself—that C.J. didn't like blue? But then I took a minute to think about the blue bear–themed first birthday party and the pink Disney Princess–themed third birthday party and realized that Matt was probably right.

Chapter 6

C.J. WAS THREE YEARS OLD and a total and complete pink-aholic. He ignored every other color, except, on occasion, purple. So much so that during his annual checkup just after his third birthday, I asked his pediatrician to test him for color blindness because at preschool he wouldn't name all of the colors. Maybe he just couldn't see the color blue; maybe he was color-blind. Maybe that would explain something, anything. The pediatrician performed a test, and it turned out that C.J. could see colors perfectly. The doctor did write in his file that C.J. refused to acknowledge the color blue. Several times I asked C.J. why he ignored the color blue and disliked it so much, but all I ever got from him in reply was a shoulder shrug. I finally gave up and shook my head in disapproval at myself because I was a mother who had her son evaluated by a doctor because he liked the color pink more than the color blue.

We were six months A.B. (After Barbie), and the sight of our son playing with girl toys had come to be less thought provoking and more commonplace. Sometimes it was easier for me to connect with C.J. over Barbie than it had ever been to connect with Chase over Thomas the Tank Engine. After all, Babs and I went way back. Playing Barbies with C.J. was much like playing Barbies with Michael. Just like Michael, C.J. would manage to tangle Barbie's hair to rat's-nest proportions and I would be left to return her snarls to smooth. Both my brother and my son have scolded me countless times for my Barbie outfit choices and styling techniques.

Matt and I were making progress in accepting and not overthinking the girl-toy issue. In fact, we were getting pretty comfortable with it because it made our son so happy.

Then C.J. started cross-dressing.

It started one day when I was I folding my clean laundry. C.J. grabbed my orange tank top with scalloped trim and ran out of the room and up the stairs. He was always sabotaging my laundry work, most often knocking over a pile of just-folded towels and laughing so hard he'd fall on the ground. I ignored the tank-top thievery, until he came downstairs wearing it as a dress with a pair of my plum-colored heels.

He entered the living room methodically and ladylike, with a happy, mischievous grin spread from ear to ear and eyes that looked dangerous with excitement. He had crossed some line. He knew it and he liked it.

Chase, who was sitting on the couch, started giggling uncontrollably and continued to do so even as he fell off the couch holding his stomach as it contracted and his crotch as he nearly peed his cargo shorts. I smiled and gave a few quiet laughs because of my son in a dress and heels standing before me, because of Chase's total-body amusement, and because I didn't know what else to do.

C.J. stayed dressed as he was for the rest of the day.

"What is he wearing?" Matt asked when he got home from work.

I had really hoped that I could get C.J. out of his getup before Matt saw him.

"My tank top and heels," I replied.

"I can see that. Thank you," Matt said. "But why is he wearing it?"

"I have no idea," I said honestly. "He likes it."

I laughed a little more quiet laughter because, again, I didn't know what else to do.

In our bedroom that night, the questions and conversations about C.J.'s behavior started all over again.

This is just a phase, right? Yes.

This isn't just a phase, right? Nope.

What do we do next? I have no idea.

Are you comfortable with him dressing up like a girl? Yes and no.

Is he gay? I wish I knew.

Is it something more? I hope not.

How concerned should we be? I don't know.

Are we overreacting? Probably, but maybe not.

I worried constantly, unnecessarily, and unprovoked about Matt and how he was doing with all of it, with his son not being a typical boy, when he himself was that personified. Would Matt's concern and questioning turn to anger, distance, or some other feeling so powerful that fleeing the situation might begin to seem like the better, easier option? Would he blame me? Was I the one to blame? I blamed me. C.J. was just like my brother. I had passed on the gene that made him a little boy who liked all things fabulous.

I have always felt like I have to be the strong one, the one who is the most okay with C.J.'s behaviors and future possibilities. Matt never asked me to take on that role. I did because I felt that it was mine for the taking. If C.J. is the way he is because of genetics, then it's my fault. The gene came from me.

Initially I was afraid that Matt would blame me and our marriage would struggle. I felt like I had to make everything as okay as possible. Eventually I realized that I was putting too much pressure on myself and wasn't giving Matt enough credit. C.J. is our child; he may present unique needs and challenges, but he is our son and they are our challenges to overcome and our needs to meet. Our son is not a deal breaker.

Shortly after the day that C.J. took my orange tank top and never gave it back, he was at Nana's house baking when he put on her black-and-white polka-dot apron and refused to take it off when it was time to leave. He wore it to bed and whenever we were at home for two weeks straight. He paired it with my red patent-leather Mary Jane heels, one of my silver bangle bracelets, and a calculator as his cell phone. He said he was "Mommy going to work."

He swiped a pastel heart–covered dish towel from a friend's kitchen counter and fastened it around his waist using one of Chase's belts. He wore pajama pants on his head, pretending that the legs were long braids hanging down. With my reluctant approval, he started getting random hand-me-down girls' clothes: a flower-girl dress from my goddaughter and Tinker Bell boots from the neighbor girl. Piece by piece his wardrobe was expanding.

C.J. dressing up like a girl at home initially felt a little unnatural to Matt and me, but not as much so as when he'd started playing with girl toys. I don't know why; you'd think it would have been the opposite. Maybe it's because over the course of several months, we had eased our way into this phase. It was a slippery slope, and we had slid slowly. Although we questioned our own judgment, we allowed our son to wear feminine articles of clothing—but only at home.

Again, we established rules. We have always referred to his girl clothes as his "dress-ups" in general or to a specific article by its specific name (e.g., his gray dress, jean skirt, pink nightgown), and we have never called his by now large assortment of feminine frocks his "real clothes" or his "girl clothes." For us they have always been about play, fantasy, imagination, and freedom. They have always been there for the wearing, without asking.

Initially, we only allowed him to wear them in the safety of our own home, because we didn't want him or Chase getting teased. Then we realized that it was just as fine for him to wear them to the homes of his grandparents and our close friends. Soon he was wearing his hot pink dress with light pink hearts on it and Tinker Bell boots to ride his scooter up and down our street. But that's as far into "public" as he ever wore "girl clothes." And the vast majority of the time, he was 100 percent fine with that. He never pushed us or campaigned to wear his girl clothes out in public.

We never wanted him to think that shopping from the girls' department was an option. We never ventured into the pink areas of fashion retailers. We had no need. I didn't want to waste money on clothes he would only wear in the privacy of our own home. I didn't want shopping experiences in the future to be lengthened by his wanting to check out yet another section. I didn't want to fight with him in the morning when getting dressed for school because he might want to wear girl clothes. On so many levels, I didn't want to have to deal with his thinking that he could shop from the girls' clothing section. I knew that I wasn't wrong. I couldn't explain it, but I knew that I just absolutely did not want to go there—shopping for girl clothes for and with my son. I let the important people in our lives know that we had drawn a line there, on the outskirts of the area with racks of skirts. We would not enter. I asked our family and friends to support and respect our decision.

Then I picked C.J. up from a day with Nana Grab Bags and he was wearing a dress from the girls' section of Target.

"It was on sale and on a rack in between the girls' and boys' departments. He didn't even notice it was from the girls' section," she said, as my dad stood there shaking his head at her for buying the dress and at C.J. for wearing it. I ignored him.

I've never in all my life been so mad at my mother. I cried at her, yelled at her, packed up the kids, and drove home. Why couldn't she be on my team instead of C.J.'s? Why wouldn't she help me? Why couldn't she see that we were struggling? Why wouldn't she honor our decisions as C.J.'s parents? Was she overcompensating for missed opportunities with Michael? Or had she too learned from her mistakes, and now she was in the right and I was in the wrong?

With time, my relationship with her healed and my emotions calmed. There were still talks and reminders about decisions Matt and I had made as parents that we expected her to support. When C.J. got a little older and the worry about him being bullied became more of a reality, she got on our team more. When Chase had his own bullying story because of his brother, she seemed to really understand the importance of our decisions. But evolutions are slow, sometimes painfully so. Nana loves her boys, though she has to be reminded of our decisions as parents regularly and she works to be a member of our team. She's more accepting of C.J.'s current effeminate behaviors and possibly gay future than she ever was of Michael's; in that and so many other things I see a victory. I see us learning from our past mistakes instead of repeating them.

Chapter 7

MATT AND I MARVELED AT just how different our sons were. We were beginning to see the power of nature over nurture. We were raising two boys in the same home, with the same parents, in much the same way. But we were getting very different results. Which is what, I'm sure, lots of parents raising multiple children of the same sex think.

I've heard other moms say things like "My older son likes basketball, but my younger son likes lacrosse" or "My older son likes math, but my younger son likes English," while I sat there quietly, thinking in a mocking tone, *Well, my older son likes Batman, but my younger son likes Barbie* or *My older son likes sports, but my younger son likes show tunes.*

We were raising a typical boy who turned us into LEGO engineers, video gamers, soccer coaches, and Nerf gun targets and a girly boy who turned us into princess stalkers, hairstyle guinea pigs, Disney aficionados, and Rachel Zoes of the Barbie world.

Our two boys have never really played with the same toys, taken the same path, had the same passions, or followed the same purposes. We've nurtured our sons in much the same way; it's their natures that are different. But it would be years before we could truly appreciate the fact that we had gotten the best of both worlds.

At first we hoped and tried to believe that C.J. was going through a phase. Then we realized that it wasn't part of a phase; it was part of him. We began to acknowledge that our son was effeminate and occasionally, to people we trusted, that he was "a girl at heart." We knew no other term for it. There was no other way for us to explain it at the time.

We also assumed that his behavior was probably an indication that he was gay. Why did we jump to assuming the sexuality of our three-year-old? Because I grew up with a boy who was effeminate and who later came out as gay. It was all I knew, and as my small mind raced to explain things, that, for me, was the logical conclusion. We didn't know any better; we just knew that C.J. wasn't a "typical boy."

I remembered my brother growing up, the parenting in our home, how it shaped him as an adult, and the promises I had made to myself to do certain things differently.

Michael was a towhead who grew into a brunet. His blue eyes, however, never changed. He has always seemed like a character from a sitcom to me. As far back as I can remember, he has been larger than life and loved by all. If it takes a village to raise a child, Michael is the court jester, mayor, therapist, stylist, and official storyteller. He's always been one of my favorite people and I know he feels the same way about me.

Since C.J. started revealing his inner princess, Michael and I have had an incalculable number of talks about our childhood and what a child like C.J.—and Michael—needs from a parent. My brother and I have grown even closer than we already were, which I never would have thought possible.

Even though I was right there growing up with Michael, I was oblivious to a lot. I started to talk to him about our childhood. Was my reality not his? Did we not have fun together? We did, he confirmed, have fun together. But I learned that he felt like he was in survival mode for much of his life. He had secrets, he had shame, and he felt as if he made every family photo ugly. All because he loved girl stuff but didn't love girls and felt like he was wrong, a freak and a mistake. My parents struggled with my brother and made some parenting mishaps along the way. I promised my brother that if either one of my boys were LGBTQ (lesbian, gay, bisexual, transgender, or questioning), I'd do things differently.

I am not saying that my parents were horrible parents. They weren't; they didn't know what they were doing any more than any of us do when a baby is placed in our arms as we are wheeled out of the hospital twenty-four hours after the most intense experience of our lives. You hold on tight and do your best—at the very least you white-knuckle it through days and weeks and months and years. Plus, it was a different time. The 1970s and 1980s weren't as gay friendly as today is. I believe my mother fully when she says that she did the best she could, and I get emotional with her when she cries and feels like a failure as a mother because of her reaction when my brother came out. Once things are said and done, they can't be unspoken or undone; it's one of life's tragedies.

For her entire life our mother went to church at least once

a week. It was there that she was taught that homosexuality is a sin, so when my brother came out, a sense of doom set in. Her boy was going to hell. She felt torn, and the grieving process commenced. There would be no daughter-in-law and no grandchildren from my brother. She wondered if she had done something to cause it. If so, could she fix it?

When she tells people her age that her son is gay, the most common response is "Oh, I'm so sorry." As if he had died. It has taught her that, among her friends, having a gay son is so horrible it warrants sympathy and condolences. At Bible study with my father, she can't mention my brother during prayer requests and praises. The only prayer that fellow Bible studiers feel comfortable saying for my brother is that he'll find a nice woman to love or abstain from love and sex altogether.

Our mother feels horrible now for showing me that having a gay family member was something to hide, for being less than brave, and for placing such importance on trying to please other people. She's said that, at times, her love for my brother, for her kids, didn't triumph over her concern about what others would think or say. She's acutely aware that her relationship with Michael has suffered because of it. We've talked about all of this, and I've promised her that I'll do better, that I won't repeat her mistakes, that the lessons she has learned will be put to use by me for the sake of her grandchildren.

A little boy who likes only girl stuff. I've seen one version of this story. It's history repeating itself, to a certain extent. I have to make sure only the good parts of the history live on; the bad parts can go to hell.

We are beyond blessed to have the support of my parents, Matt's parents, a tight-knit group of friends, and, most important, Michael.

He dreams big for his nephews, and he worries about Chase and C.J. just as much as Matt and I do. He helped convince me that C.J.'s "girl-toy thing" was just a phase and that he would be tackling things like miniature bulldozers and bug robots in no time.

"Why did you, of all people, try to convince us that it was just a phase?" I asked him years later with the honesty of two glasses of wine.

"I was scared. I was really just hoping it was a phase," he said. "Listen, I know that if, in fact, what you were feeling is true, he's going to have to face the same bigotry, hate, fear, and torment I faced. And that is devastating for me."

Michael doesn't want either of his nephews to ever know that people are ugly. He doesn't want them to be called "fag," "gay," "sissy," and "fairy" by the kids in school and in the neighborhood while adults stand by idly and think, *Well, he's gotta learn. He's gotta man up.* He doesn't want Chase or C.J. to have to have thick skin.

Michael once wrote to me, "As C.J. continued to not phase out of his fantastically pink phase, I began to realize that C.J. and I are different. You and Matt are going to raise him to be proud of who he is, to relish his creative use of purple, pink and all the other nongray colors. He feels safe to twirl, flit, flip, skip and bounce. C.J. has what I didn't have. C.J. has a home that loves him for who he is, not who they want him to be. To say you and Matt are fantastic parents is like saying the Grand Canyon is huge. It's obvious. You have effortlessly created an environment that is at once safe and fun, yet disciplined and structured."

His words touched me, and they felt so good. Sometimes we all need to be told that we are not failing—especially parents. I started to question all of the rules and compromises we had put into place when it came to C.J. He was three years and four months old, and we were letting him take "girl toys" with him more liberally but still pretty much on a case-by-case basis. We made sure that all remnants of "girls' clothes" were off him before we left the house, including accessories and socks.

But we never made Chase leave his toys at the house or in the car. Why weren't we extending the same courtesy to C.J.? What were we teaching our sons? Was C.J.'s love for all things girly something to be ashamed of and to hide? Were the opinions of others really that important? Was he free to be who he was created to be, but only at home?

We weren't parenting fairly, and it started to drive me crazy.

I talked it over with Matt and he agreed. We had two boys whom we had thought we would parent the same, but we couldn't, so we had to adjust and evolve. We were tired of being hypervigilant and bargaining. We wanted to leave the house and run an errand without thinking about it and scanning our son for prohibited items. We had become more concerned about the opinions of strangers than about parenting C.J. to the best of our ability. We decided to make a change, to parent our sons equally and fairly, and to let C.J. take his "girl things" out of hiding and out of our home.

We made the change and were met with every kind of reaction from every kind of person: questioning stares, dirty looks, disgusted head shakes, knowing nods, and smiles of encouragement. C.J. was too happy and too young to notice the feelings he provoked in others. Since we changed the way we parent him, C.J. has been his happiest. We haven't always been, but as parents, we wouldn't have it any other way. It took time, but eventually we all started to feel free and liberated.

Chapter 8

WE HAD SHIFTED OUR parenting perspective, and we were ready to start enjoying summer with our sons, who were both free to follow their fancies. Then we realized that the rest of our community was behind in the evolution. Humans want to categorize things to better understand them, but our son and his behaviors can't be easily categorized. Our family's defying the norms, crossing the lines, and living outside of boxes made people uncomfortable and our lives more difficult at times. It seemed that every time we were content and felt like we were thriving as a family, something or someone would remind us that how we were choosing to raise our son was not the norm. When everybody in Orange County was racing to keep up with the Joneses, we were anything but the Joneses. It became glaringly obvious.

Simple things like going to McDonald's made us feel different. McDonald's meals and McNuggets have been making kids happy for decades. Based on my own childhood experiences, I thought that a child's heart—or at least fifteen minutes of content quiet—could be purchased with a Happy Meal. Then I had a child whose heart was neither all boy nor all girl, and

McDonald's started handing out its kids' meals based on gender. That is when, suddenly, Happy Meals weren't so happy.

C.J. doesn't want a Tonka Garage Truck, a Hot Wheels Battle Force 5 Fused car, or a Young Justice action figure; he wants a My Little Pony, a Barbie: A Fairy Secret doll, or a Littlest Pet Shop pet. But what C.J. wants totally confuses McDonald's. That's how I learned that a simple thing like lunch can be complicated when my son is at the table.

We walked into McDonald's and ordered a Happy Meal to take with us to the beach.

"For a boy, right?" the cashier asked, looking at C.J.

"It's for a boy, but we would like the girl toy," I explained.

The cashier stared at me, then at C.J., then back at me. I smiled back at him. He stared at me. Because of C.J., I was learning to give different kinds of smiles that said different things. The one I gave next said, *We want a girl toy. Is that a problem? Can I help you with something?*

C.J. looked back and forth between the cashier and me. His eyes told me that he was fearful that his request for a girl toy might be rejected because he is—obviously—a boy. He wasn't concerned with what the cashier thought—he wasn't to that point in his own development yet—he just wanted, like every three-year-old child, to get what he wanted. Tears were averted, and he breathed a sigh of relief when his wish was granted.

A few weeks later, with Matt at the wheel, we drove up to a McDonald's and ordered a Happy Meal.

"For a boy or a girl?" the bored voice mumbled out of the metal drive-through box.

"It's for a girl," Matt said, upset that gender identity issues were now being served with his Big Mac.

As wonderful as Matt has been about raising a boy who only likes girl stuff, it is hard for him to refer to C.J. as a she. As we sat in our car in the drive-through line, I pointed out that he didn't have to refer to C.J. as a girl; he could have selected his words differently. I had gotten used to being very specific when I placed the order. I always ordered a Happy Meal with chicken nuggets, apple juice, and a Barbie, or whatever the "girl" option was for the month. I refused to say "girl toy" or that it was for a girl.

Matt gripped the steering wheel a little tighter. I started to smile, as I often do when he's frustrated and I can tell that he doesn't want to talk about it and just wants things to not be a pain in the ass. Chase smiled and rolled his eyes in the backseat. I would soon find out that we weren't the only family dealing with such McProblems.

The very next day, my college friend Colleen posted about McDonald's on her Facebook page: "I don't like that when ordering a Happy Meal I'm asked if it is for a boy or a girl, when the question should actually be 'do you want a car or a Barbie?'"

I agreed and waited to see what her other friends on Facebook would say. A handful of her mom friends felt the same way. Colleen's little guy didn't like girl stuff the way C.J. liked girl stuff, but she explained that "other than the obvious obnoxiousness of the gender stereotyping going on, sometimes the 'opposite gender' toy is the better choice for my son. He knows what a stuffed bear is, not so much a Bakugan whosiewhatsit."

On one trip to the Golden Arches, Chase saw on his Happy Meal box that there was a Happy Meal website with fun games and activities. When we got home, we pulled up the site and started to register to play. McDonald's, again, wanted to know if we were a boy or a girl. I couldn't explain to the computer that we had one boy who likes to play with boy stuff and one boy who likes to play with girl stuff. We logged off and I walked away knowing that if McDonald's kept up this separate-genders nonsense, I would have to make lunch at home more often. Nobody in our family wanted that, especially me.

I was talking to another mom about our fast-food drama and she informed me that we shouldn't be going to McDonald's so much anyway. We should be doing more picnics at the park, where we could eat and play, just like at McDonald's but for less money and with healthier food. I was familiar with this "healthier child" concept; I had, in the past, heard other moms talking about how their kids were in grade school and had never even eaten at McDonald's. It was a foreign notion to me; I hadn't been raised that way. There was a McDonald's around the corner from our house growing up and we could be found there often. But then again, here I was trying to make positive changes for my kids' sake, so we laid off Mickey D's.

A few days later, we were at one of the "it" parks in South Orange County. A place where anyone who is anyone play-dates. A place where the South Orange County Mommy Mafia arrives in True Religion jeans carrying Coach purses, Starbucks, and BPA-free sippy cups.

It's not our normal scene. But my friend said it should be and my boys dig the park. So we went, with no clique, no mommy entourage, no nanny in tow, no organic snacks. We are rebels, me and my boys.

The park was hopping and we were doing our thing. C.J. climbed to the top of the highest play structure, which looked like a castle with slide offshoots, firefighter-style poles to slide down, and staircases galore.

"Maaaaa-meeeeeeeeee!" he yelled from the highest perch.

There were so many kids at the park that day yelling the word "Mommy" that I had gotten numb to it. I didn't even hear C.J. calling me.

"Maaaaaa-meeeeeeeee!" he yelled even louder.

Everyone was looking in my direction, judging, as I, oblivious, continued my inner monologue about the size of my thighs, jeggings, and whether it was okay to shop at Forever 21 after the age of thirty-one. Chase came over to me.

"MOM! C.J. is calling you!" he alerted me.

I snapped out of my internal conflict, looked up at C.J., and waved, just as he, in his loudest outside voice, screamed a declaration: "I'm a princess! The most beautiful princess in all the land. I'm Rapunzel letting down my hair."

He proceeded to let his imaginary yards of tendrils down the side of the tower.

Gasps and giggles galore came from the South Orange County Mommy Mafia and their little maniacs.

"Yes, you are, baby!" I shouted back in support while giving the other moms a smug, proud look. *Who cares if my son is the most beautiful princess in all the land?* I reasoned with myself.

But that day, Chase did. He cared. He looked at me, horrified. He was getting ready to enter the second grade and was becoming more aware of other people's judgments, gossiping tendencies, and bullying. He wanted to leave the park immediately. I gave him the standard "five more minutes" warning, and he sulked on a bench for all of them. When we got in the car, he was upset.

"I'm sorry," I said as I thought that had C.J. been pretending to be a prince, none of this would have happened. If a little girl had been pretending to be a prince, people would have applauded her in their minds for being empowered. How come when girls play with gender it's a sign of strength and when boys play with gender it's a sign of weakness? I could slap whoever made our society that way.

It was quiet as we drove home, and I realized that oftentimes at that point, C.J.'s failure to comply with traditional gender norms affected C.J. the least of anybody. His behaviors and preferences were affecting us—his mom, dad, and brother—the most, because we had been on this earth long enough to learn what judgment, insult, and mockery look, feel, and sound like.

Chase wouldn't talk to me about it, but he would talk to Matt.

"The kids tease me because my brother likes girl stuff. They ask me every day if he is still into girl stuff, and when I tell them yes, they run away from me and tease me on the playground," he said, fighting back tears. It was the first we were hearing of this.

"Why don't you just tell them no, that he's not into girl stuff anymore?" Matt said.

"Because that would be lying, and you told me never to lie."

Tough-as-hell parenting moment number 5,763.

Matt told Chase that it's okay to give someone a not-totally-truthful answer when it really is none of their business and in the name of self-protection. He tried to explain that there is a difference between keeping a secret and keeping something private.

"Celebrities do it all the time," I interjected as I entered the room. Of course I was eavesdropping, and now I was trying to put it into terms that Chase might understand, because we do watch *E! News* one or two nights a week during bath time.

Matt looked at me like I was a lunatic. I remembered a lesson I learned from attending PFLAG (Parents and Friends of Lesbians and Gays) meetings when I was in my twenties. PFLAG is a nonprofit organization that was founded in 1973 for parents, families, friends, and straight allies to unite with LGBTQ people in a shared mission of support, education, and advocacy. It's the most supportive support group I've ever seen; it's good for my soul; it's what church should feel like. PFLAG teaches you that when a person comes out of the closet, so must his or her loved ones, in their own time. C.J.—at this point—was living an "out" life. He was living his life exactly as he wanted to live it, with no secrets, no hiding, and no care for social norms. Matt and I as parents had made a conscious decision to follow his lead and live that way as well. But C.J.'s unabashed way of life was beginning to make Chase feel embarrassed, uncomfortable, and even angry, at inopportune times and in less-than-ideal locations. A new parenting struggle was just beginning and, again, it was one that we hadn't completely expected.

We had already started to worry incessantly about C.J. getting bullied for his effeminate ways. It caught us off guard when we realized that we had to worry about Chase getting teased and bullied because of them too.

Feeling that Chase was in need of some extra love and

attention that week, we invited his new friend over to play for an entire day. One hour before the coolest kid in the neighborhood was to arrive at our house, we were running around discreetly hiding all of C.J.'s girl toys to save Chase from possible embarrassment and ridicule. As we stashed Strawberry Shortcake out of sight, Matt and I wondered whether, while protecting Chase, we were teaching C.J. to hide his true self. We felt like we couldn't win, like we couldn't please everyone at any one given time, like we were always squashing one of our sons' spirits while trying to honor the spirit of the other.

We considered that we could seize the opportunity to teach someone else's child about celebrating uniqueness in others. We could leave the girl toys in plain view and explain to Chase's new friend that people are different and in our house that is perfectly okay. But was that our place?

A lesson we have learned from C.J. is that sometimes we don't owe anybody answers, sometimes we don't have answers, and sometimes we lie like celebrities.

Chapter 9

SUMMER ENDED, AND IN September C.J. returned to pre-school and Chase entered the second grade. By September of our effeminate son's third year, he had informed us that he was going to be Snow White for Halloween. He said it matter-of-factly, yet still I stuttered and stammered for an answer or an excuse not to let my son dress up as a girl for Halloween and leave the house and knock on the doors of strangers to ask for candy for the entire neighborhood and all of the local schoolkids and their parents to see. To us, that felt like taking this whole thing too far, like we'd be parading our son around and asking for problems. That was a line we weren't ready to cross.

I Googled a bunch of random phrase combos, trying to fit a life dilemma into a search bar. Boys dressing as girls for Halloween. My son wants to be a princess for Halloween. Boys as Snow White. Boys as Disney Princesses. Should I let my three-year-old son be Snow White for Halloween. Gender-neutral Halloween costumes.

Not much turned up with those search terms, so I got search happy. Boys playing with girls' toys. Boys dressing as

girls. Boys liking girls' things. What are the chances of an effeminate boy growing up to be gay? Little gay boys. Raising a
gay child. Is my child gay?

I had never dared to open the Internet in search of information on kids like C.J. But once I started, I couldn't stop.
Not much was turning up, though. I gave up on Google and
moved on to popular parenting sites and mom blogs. But there
weren't sections within the parenting sites I visited or dedi-
cated mom blogs for people raising a child like mine. I desperately wanted to connect and get some answers. I realized that
we were feeling alone and isolated.

I complained to my brother.

"Well, babe, you can't be the only parent out there looking
for info like this. You should start your own blog. Be the site,
the resource that you want but can't find. You're a smart girl
and a great writer. You should do it," he said.

The thought scared the hell out of me. I wanted other people to share their lives with me; I didn't want to share my life
with other people. I wanted to be a voyeur from the safety of
my own home, cloaked in anonymity and baggy sweatpants. I
didn't want to rock the boat.

I couldn't stop thinking about it or refining my search
terms in hopes of finding a place to connect. I couldn't possibly have found a gaping, empty hole in the Internet. I thought
that there was a place for everybody, with no community left
to be created. The lack of camaraderie and my brother's prod-
ding eventually set me in motion.

During the month of October, I spent my time thinking
about becoming a blogger and working on a costume for
C.J. that was a compromise. I got to the bottom of what C.J.

wanted most out of a Halloween costume, which was to wear makeup and fabric that felt nice. I sat him on my lap in front of the computer and went to a popular website for Halloween costumes. I clicked on the "Boys' Costumes" section of the site and tricked C.J. into thinking that those costumes were his only options. Again, I was hiding half of the world from him, and I felt guilty about it. But it also felt like something I had to do to protect both of my boys from what other people might think and say and to keep the holiday as drama-free as possible.

We ended up settling on a black satiny polyester-blend skeleton costume with a face full of black and white makeup, including black lipstick that would have impressed the girls and boys working the MAC counter.

In between costume compromises, I moved forward with starting a blog. I couldn't stop thinking about it and what my brother had said—I couldn't be the only parent out there looking for information about raising a child like C.J. I picked a name for it, created a strategic plan for it (I'm type A, I know), and started writing, but not publishing.

I talked to Matt about it.

"I'm cool with you doing it, but you better be careful," he said.

What the hell did that mean? I better be careful? As if I were cliff diving or tightrope walking or running in six-inch heels. He implied that there was danger. I got scared again. I didn't want to expose my family to others, to harm, or to consequences that might haunt us for years to come—like C.J. hating me when he got older and learned that I had written about his liking dolls.

Matt and I ironed out some details. I assured him that I would write anonymously and photos would never show faces. He wanted to read and have final approval of every post before it was published.

Deal.

I talked to one of my best friends, Marie, about it.

"I think you should do it. You've never cared about what people think, and you're the best writer I know. You better do it. I'm going to hold you accountable," Marie said as we watched her daughter Grace and C.J. play at the park one day.

I think that subconsciously that's why I told her. I knew she'd hold me accountable; she'd make me do it. If she saw value in it, she wouldn't let me give up.

I was worried about being perceived as outing my child. I was worried about haters, criticism, and people telling me that I was a bad parent. I was afraid of the repercussions, the exposure, and the commitment. What would people say? I had learned to live my life not caring what people said or thought; then I had C.J. and suddenly I started giving a shit again. Where had my bravery and fearlessness gone? I needed to do this. I needed to share our lives in order to meet other families who had lived or were living similar lives. I needed to do it so that I wouldn't feel so damn alone. I was getting my nerve up.

Then, out of nowhere, came the blogger Sarah Manley and her famous "My Son Is Gay" post about her son dressing up as Daphne from *Scooby-Doo* for Halloween and the judgmental, bullying, disdainful reactions he got from the disapproving moms at his religious preschool.

"My son is gay. Or he's not. I don't care. He is still my son. And he is 5. And I am his mother. And if you have a problem with anything mentioned above, I don't want to know you," Sarah wrote on her *Nerdy Apple* blog.

I obviously got excited. This mom was going to share all about her little LGBTQer with the whole world, and I wasn't going to have to. I could cyberstalk her in my moments of downtime instead of managing and writing my own blog in the free time I didn't have.

Then she went back to writing content more typical of a mom blog, and I felt deflated. I wanted to read more about her boy Boo. I felt like I was so close to finding a mom, child, and blog that I could relate to. What was wrong with this woman? Didn't she understand that she had gotten my hopes up and then sent them crashing down? In my need to get more from Sarah and her post, I started to read every single comment posted by readers in response to her story, both on her blog and elsewhere. After all, her blog post had gone insanely viral. It was everywhere. Everybody was talking about it. Four million people have read the post and more than forty-seven thousand comments have been made in response.

Holy shit, some people were mean. Evil, evil stuff was written about Sarah and her son. It crushed me to read some of the comments. I felt bad for her. And it felt like every attack on her and her son was a direct attack on my son and me. I took it all so personally that I couldn't sleep at night and had a hard time concentrating on anything else while awake. Why were this woman and her son and their story affecting me so much? Because they were us. I had never read anything that so closely resembled our lives before. For once, I didn't feel so alone.

Months later I had the opportunity to hear Sarah speak on a panel at a conference for women bloggers. She was witty, smart, a smart-ass, and well read; basically she was everything that I look for in a friend. Eventually, I got in touch with her via e-mail and was able to learn more about her, her family, her blog, and the aftermath of the blog post read round the world.

Our stories were similar in a lot of ways. We're both married to cops; we both like to read and write; we're both proud moms who don't like injustices, bullies, or crappy people.

Sarah had been blogging for four years before she wrote the "My Son Is Gay" post. She had started blogging because it was an easy way to communicate with her friends and family all at once.

"When you wrote that post, did you know, feel, like it was going to be something big, get attention? What did you expect?" I asked her.

"Nothing. I expected nothing. It felt cathartic to get my feelings out. Best case, I thought maybe a dozen people would read it. *Holy hell!* It went viral fast. There was a CNN interview, the *Today* show trip, radio and TV requests; it was reposted pretty much everywhere—more than eight hundred thousand times on Facebook alone. And we had a bit of trouble with the church that Boo's preschool was affiliated with," Sarah said.

"I read some of the negative stuff people wrote about you. . . ." I trailed off.

"I had several hateful comments and a few wackadoo e-mails. I don't respond to hate mail. I feel the hate is a reflection of the one spewing it. It doesn't reflect on me. I know I love my kids, and they certainly know I love them," she said.

"Did you ever feel like unpublishing the post? Just removing it to not have to deal with the haters?" I asked.

"When it first started going viral, I was freaked out. I didn't regret posting it, but I was nervous about all of the attention. The negative comments and e-mails mostly made me just shake my head, and I didn't consider taking it down. I felt like I had to stand by my words. If they meant that much to so many people, parents, adult gays, teens, et cetera, I had to make sure that I meant what I said and could articulate to the detractors that I was a reasonable person, not some kook looking for attention."

I've learned that Sarah's son Boo isn't a girly boy; he's just a boy who wanted to dress like a girl for Halloween, and she allowed it. She considers him more gender neutral, not particularly masculine or feminine leaning.

"I felt a little weird about us getting lumped in with gender-bending kids. Not because I was disapproving in any way, but I think my situation was *very* different. I feel like many people have much more difficult situations than mine and felt that I did a bit of a disservice to them. My son wore a costume on Halloween. That was very black and white. People that actually deal with gender issues and kids every day have it much rougher. I didn't want to come across as a sham, if that makes sense. I felt like our situation should have been presented in the media as a bullying issue, especially the fact that it was from adults—mothers—to a child, thus being a textbook example of how bullying is a cycle that is all too often learned at home," Sarah said.

For a long time, as many positive comments as Sarah got,

I could focus only on the negative ones. They hit so close to home, felt so personal. Part of me just wanted to be thankful that she had written about her young son being gay, that I could see the hate in the world that I would have had to endure had I been the first to write a post like that and move on with my life. But I couldn't. I sat on the sidelines and watched what happened to Sarah for two months. She was everywhere: Internet, television, radio, print. She had sparked a national debate about LGBTQ kids, when really she had intended to make a statement about bullying.

But eventually, I started to feel the pull, again, to start a blog about the adventures in raising a possibly LGBTQ child. There was still a gaping hole in the Internet, as far as I was concerned. Two quotes kept popping up in my mind:

> *Well-behaved women seldom make history.*
> —LAUREL THATCHER ULRICH

> *Why not? Why not you? Why not now?*
> —ASLAN THE LION, *The Chronicles of Narnia*

Why was I behaving this way? Why was I waiting for someone else to do something that I steadfastly felt needed to be done? What was wrong with me? That's not the kind of woman or mother I wanted to be.

Chapter 10

❀

THE HOLIDAY SEASON WAS QUICKLY upon us, and I couldn't stop thinking about the blog and debating its potential. Then an event happened that made me know for sure that I had to do something.

C.J. climbed onto Santa's lap, nervously twiddling his fingers. It was the moment he had been anticipating for weeks.

"What do you want for Christmas, little boy?" Santa asked.

"Disney's *Tangled* Rapunzel Braiding Friends Hair Braider," my son said with a heavy lisp and the speed of an auctioneer.

Santa looked to me for help.

"Disney's *Tangled* Rapunzel Braiding Friends Hair Braider," I offered.

Insert strange look from Santa in my direction. Insert strange look from Santa in my son's direction.

"What else do you want?" the Fat Man asked, hoping for a more gender-appropriate answer.

"Dat's it. Just *Tangled*."

The wannabe-elf photographer snickered at me. I didn't like the tone of her snicker.

Please understand how truly fabulous the Disney's *Tangled*

Rapunzel Braiding Friends Hair Braider was (even if it is a mouthful).

It's a Barbie-sized Rapunzel doll with hair longer than she is tall. She comes with a stand that you put her in, and the stand has three cute animal friends on it. You put a section of Rapunzel's hair in the hands of each animal friend, you turn a crank, and they braid Rapunzel's hair. It's pretty amazing.

Ten days later it was Christmas morning, and as C.J. unwrapped Disney's *Tangled* Rapunzel Braiding Friends Hair Braider, squeals of delight could be heard in every part of the world where Santa's sleigh had traveled. The hair braider didn't leave his proud grip for weeks.

Some people who got wind of C.J.'s Christmas wish list advised against getting him "girl toys." I considered it, for about one second. The gifts we had given him the year before missed the mark. We remembered his disappointment and weren't going to let it happen again. People kept asking us what we were going to do. As if C.J.'s wanting only "girl toys" for Christmas was the biggest catastrophe since the inn had no room.

Christmas is for the children. (Okay, I know, it's really for the birth of Christ, the Son of God. But besides that, it's for the children.) It's for getting a child the toy he or she has been dreaming about from the pages of the toy catalog that is falling apart from wear. That's how it was for me when I was young, and that's how I'm raising my children. Poor Michael used to sit next to me under the Christmas tree for pictures, holding a football and staring at the Barbie in my hands. He had Christmas morning envy. My son wouldn't have that, not this year or ever again. Michael didn't always feel comfortable asking Santa or our mother for the gifts he really wanted; C.J. is unabashed in his requests. My mother and father might not have always felt comfortable fulfilling the requests my brother did voice. I worked to get comfortable, get over it, and get my son the doll that was at the top of his wish list.

I offered no apologies to anyone for the "girl toys" on C.J.'s Christmas wish list, not to Santa, not to his elf, not even to the old hag in the mall who shook her head in disgust when she spotted C.J. dancing in the food court with his *Tangled* doll to Ke$ha's "Tik Tok" the day after Christmas when we were hitting the sales.

My only regret about giving C.J. the Disney's *Tangled* Rapunzel Braiding Friends Hair Braider was that the twelve-inch hair turned into an enormous, elaborate knot at least once a day, which evoked tears and pleas for me to "make her back to pretty," which usually required more braids than Bo Derek sported in *10*. Other than that, Matt and I knew that we had given our son the best gift of his life: Rapunzel and the support to be who he was created to be.

It had been more than a year since C.J. started liking girl stuff, and we more fully acknowledged that he was special and different. More important, we agreed that our role as his parents was not to change him but to love him. We also knew that we had to do everything in our power to make the world a more accepting place for both of our sons.

As the glittery ball dropped in Times Square and 2011 peeked its tentative head into our conservative Orange County neighborhood, I quietly launched RaisingMyRainbow.com as the first "mommy blog" to chronicle the daily joys, struggles, and, sometimes, embarrassments of raising a gender-creative child.

It started off with the tagline "Adventures in raising a slightly effeminate, possibly gay, totally fabulous son," because at the time I didn't know any better than to equate effeminacy in our son with his sexuality.

As written in my blog's strategic plan (I'm such a dork sometimes; it reminds me of when I was little and would line up my Cabbage Patch Kids, each with a piece of paper and a pencil, pretend that they were my secretaries and I was the CEO, and dictate memos to them about how only Lisa Frank office supplies were allowed at our offices), I started Raising MyRainbow.com for myself. To record my feelings and experiences, like any blogger, but not to rant or stand on a cyber-soapbox or be sensationalistic. I realized that I was advocating, but I didn't want to be a sit-in-stand-up-picket-sign-protester advocate; I wanted to offer people an honest and heartfelt glimpse into our lives and urge them to shift their perceptions in our favor or at least be a little more open to people who are different.

I also started the blog for any other person in a situation similar to ours, raising a child like ours. There had to be more of us out there, right? Right?! We need support, to hear other people's stories and know that we aren't alone.

And I started it in hopes that I would draw an LGBTQ audience, because they are the ones who have the answers to a lot of my questions about raising a child like mine. Such as: When did you know you were different? When did you know you were gay? Did you do this? Did you do that? How did your parents treat you? How do you wish they had treated you? How did your peers treat you? What can I do for my son that you wish someone had done for you? What city has the best Pride festivities?

My audience wasn't going to be everybody. I understood that all too well. Initially I felt as if I were in hiding after publishing a post. I hoped that people would read it but not know that I was the author behind it. I was afraid of being recognized out in public, even though my blog contained no identifying photos or names. I wanted to be an anonymous performer in front of a large audience. I wanted to create change but get no credit.

Back in the beginning days of my blog, if a hundred people read a post, I felt like a total and complete rock star (one in hiding who was terrified of celebrity, mind you). I started to hear from people who weren't comfortable with my blog's content, my son, or my parenting. But for every e-mail or comment of opposition, I received about a dozen of support and encouragement. In the beginning, the hateful responses to my writing would fill me with anger and annoyance that made it hard to sleep. I dabbled in the mean world of Tylenol PM, and when that didn't work, I'd formulate responses meant to cut the opponents to shreds and then hit the delete button, never sending them. Soon I got numb to the hate while embracing the love. I quit wasting my time on wastes of human potential.

Almost immediately, my readers helped to educate me, sometimes politely, sometimes not, but I got an education nonetheless. When I started writing, I knew I had an effeminate son who we assumed was gay. I didn't know that I had a gender-creative, gender-nonconforming, gender-variant son with gender dysphoria and/or gender identity disorder. I wasn't hip to the lingo. A few weeks in, I learned—and felt a little dumb, but also thankful that my son's behavior was starting to make more sense, or at least have an explanation.

Although I knew the difference between gender and sexuality, I had it reinforced by readers time and time again. I still do. I don't mind. A person's sex is about what's in their pants, their gender is about what's in their brain, and their sexuality is about what's in their heart.

In other words, a person's sex is either male or female based on their genitalia/reproductive organs, internal and external. If you have a penis, your sex is male. If you have a vagina, your sex is female. If you display sexual characteristics of both sexes, then you are intersex.

A person's gender can be male or female based on what their brain tells them they are, or their brain can tell them that they are neither all male nor all female but some combination of the two or that they don't belong to either gender at all. My brain tells me I'm female. It's simple for me and for most people, but it isn't for everyone.

A person's sexuality can be heterosexual if their heart (and genetic makeup, I'll argue to the day I die) tells them to love a person of the opposite sex. A person's sexuality can be homosexual if their heart (and genetic makeup) tells them to love a person of the same sex. There are also many people who don't fall neatly into one of these two categories. And that's okay.

Have I considered that C.J. may be transgender, that his sex is male while his gender is female? That maybe he was born in the wrong body? Yes. It's hard to see a boy with a perfect mani-pedi, in a cheerleader skirt, waving pom-poms, and not consider it. Go ahead, try. Have I considered that he is pre-homosexual? Absolutely. I grew up with a brother who, looking back, had gender-nonconforming tendencies and later came out as gay. My initial, uneducated conclusion could still prove true. Statistically speaking, 60 to 80 percent of gender-nonconforming little boys grow up to be members of the LGBTQ community.

My readers and my further research finally helped me to give a name to C.J.'s disconnect between sex and gender. It was a life-changing moment when I read the definition of "childhood gender nonconformity" on Wikipedia:

> Childhood gender nonconformity is a phenomenon in which pre-pubescent children do not conform to expected gender-related sociological or psychological patterns, and/or identify with the opposite gender. Typical behaviour among those who exhibit the phenomenon includes but is not limited to a propensity to cross-dress, refusal to take part in activities conventionally thought suitable for the gender and the exclusive choice of play-mates of the opposite sex.
>
> Multiple studies have correlated childhood gender non-conformity with eventual gay/bisexual and transgender outcomes. In some studies, a majority of those who identify as gay or lesbian self-report being gender non-conforming as children. However, the accuracy of these studies has been questioned from within the academic community. The therapeutic community is currently divided on the proper response to childhood gender non-conformity. One study suggested that childhood gender non-conformity is heritable.

That was it. Spot-on. We had been living and, sometimes, struggling with it for more than a year, and now it had a name. Our son is gender nonconforming. A weight had been lifted off our shoulders: there was a name for C.J.'s behaviors and way of life. Another weight had been placed on our shoulders: now what? Giving a challenge a name doesn't make it any less challenging.

As far as his sex goes, for now C.J. self-identifies as a boy. He slides on the gender spectrum at his leisure depending on the day, the outfit, and the occasion.

Sometimes I think, *He really is a girl at heart,* and then he'll release the rankest fart and laugh, ask to keep a dead lizard as a pet, or tell me that he loves his wiener so much that he wants me to kiss it. Sometimes I'll refer to him as my son, and then he'll enter the room wearing a nightgown, a tiara, lip gloss, and long black satin gloves and carrying a purse. The joke is always on me. Just when I think I know my child, he surprises me.

Chapter 11

ONCE MATT AND I HAD a name and a definition—other than our own—for C.J.'s behaviors, it was easier to explain him to others, especially Chase.

Chase is our easy child but not our forgotten child. He is our special firstborn who made us parents and taught us that we have no idea what we're doing when it comes to raising children. He's a handsome guy with hazel eyes that are more blue than green and shimmery light brown hair that I should probably cut more often, but he isn't overly concerned about it, so neither am I. He doesn't sweat the small stuff. He's tall for his age and has suddenly developed the huskiness of his father's side of the family. He prefers to wear dark colors and not stand out (another reason why his hand-me-down clothes aren't C.J.'s favorites).

He's gender conforming but not hypermasculine. He's a renaissance man. After a two-year relationship, he broke up with LEGOs. My bare feet were ecstatic. If I never step on a LEGO again, it will be too soon. Chase's focus is now on his Xbox, computer games, flag football, his iPod Touch, and science experiments. He likes to create and invent. He wants to take a sewing class to make pajama pants with flames on them, an art class to make a Sonic the Hedgehog collage, and a computer class to make his own video games.

As for his future career, he wants to be a chef and have his own restaurant called the Greasy Dream. He keeps a journal, not of his thoughts and life events but of his inventions and recipes. He recently wrote a recipe for Garden Island Soup. We went to the store, bought the ingredients, and prepared it. It was so surprisingly good that we made it once a week for a month.

He also is fascinated by technology and can figure out computer programs quickly. Last school year, his teacher had planned on rotating the students in the role of the classroom's "IT Support Helper." Once Chase got his shot at the spot, he stayed in it all year, helping the other kids and parent volunteers on the four classroom computers. He's taken on the role at home too. Nobody knows our many Apple products better than Chase.

Chase is happy-go-lucky and seems to be perpetually "just chillin'." He's never frantic or panicked, which makes it hard to believe that he came from me. There isn't a mean or rude bone in his body. I'm often told that he is the most polite kid to roam the playground. He's a calming force in a house of two strong-willed divas and a macho dad.

When Chase was six and seven, his feelings about C.J.'s gender nonconformity went in waves. He would notice certain things C.J. did or clothes he would wear and get angry and frustrated. Then some days he wouldn't seem to notice or care at all. Sometimes he'd say things like "Why does C.J. always have to play with girl toys?" and "When is C.J. going to start acting more like a boy?" He loved his brother, and for months he'd be fine with C.J.'s effeminate ways and then, suddenly, he would have had enough and act out. It was usually a result of the judgments or reactions of others. There were plenty of times when I felt torn between fully letting C.J. be C.J. and wanting him to conform a little in certain circumstances for Chase's sake.

Right around the time Chase turned eight, he got better about C.J.'s gender nonconformity—because we finally explained it to him. One day not long after we associated the term "gender nonconforming" with C.J., we sat Chase down and told him that there is a name for kids like C.J. They are gender nonconforming. They are boys who like girl stuff and girls who like boy stuff.

It seemed to lift a big, confusing weight off Chase's shoulders. It freed up some space in his brain and heart. There was a reason for C.J.'s being the way he was. There was a name for it. It made sense. Sometimes, when something has a name it changes things. Especially when the name is big, long, and official-sounding, like "gender nonconforming."

Weeks later I took the kids to the park to burn off some energy. Chase was practicing some of his parkour-meets-Jackie-Chan-meets-eight-year-old-white-boy-from-the-O.C. moves while C.J. played with a pink-and-yellow My Little Pony under one of the slides. Another boy ran up to the playground and called out to Chase. Turns out they were in the same class, and the boy's name was Kyle.

"Your brother is playing with a girl toy!" Kyle said to Chase after a few minutes.

"Yeah, I know, he's gender nonconforming," Chase said,

stating the facts and moving on up the ladder to the tallest slide.

"Oh," Kyle said, following Chase up the ladder. He obviously didn't understand what the term "gender nonconforming" meant, but it apparently explained why C.J. was playing with a My Little Pony, and so Kyle moved on. That was that.

Are we all just looking for an explanation? Even if we don't understand it?

I realized that I had been holding my breath, partially to hear better and partially because I panic a little at times like those. They are situations that we find ourselves in regularly and that have the potential to go all sorts of sideways.

I resumed my normal breathing pattern and took a moment to relish in the pride I was feeling because I had a kid as kick-ass as Chase, who was beginning to more fully accept, defend, and protect his girly little brother. Once he learned that what his brother was had a name and a definition and that there were other kids like him in the world, there was less shame, fear, frustration, and hesitation in Chase's life.

It hit me that day at the park: when something is out in the open, when the mystery is gone, when it is a known fact and has a name, does the power shift back into the hands of the rightful owner?

For a moment, Kyle had seemingly held the power. He saw a child doing something "different" and alerted others for the sake of amusement and attention. He thought, foolishly, that he was the first ever to do so. He was mistaken. We had lived through nearly two and a half years of people laughing at C.J.'s defiance of traditional gender norms and pointing it out to others with less-than-positive intentions.

When Chase didn't react the way Kyle expected, when he gave C.J.'s behavior a legit name and then not a second thought, the power shifted back into our favor. When we unabashedly own our differences, we shed our weakness and cloak ourselves in power. It feels damn good. We wear power well, if I do say so myself.

I went to my regular PFLAG meeting that week. How times had changed. When I first started going to PFLAG a decade ago, in support of my brother, I was the youngest attendee by far (it was another perk of attending).

Now my PFLAG family includes junior-high and high-school students who have to fit the meeting in between homework, athletic practice, tutoring, dinner, and bedtime. There are brave kids sitting in our circle who came out to their families at ages eleven, twelve, and thirteen after knowing since early elementary school that they were gay.

Most of these kids and others whom I have met outside of PFLAG decided to be out at school to shift the power back in their favor. Secrets give power to the person holding the "truth," who could possibly expose it. The powerless are the people whom the secret belongs to, the person who is scared to death (sometimes quite literally) of the secret being exposed.

The bullies, predators, haters, and gossips in life move in circles; they sniff out the smallest scent of fear and strike. When there is no fear, no secrets to sniff out and uncover, those people lose their power. The power goes back to the rightful owner.

It felt like my family was regaining some power, or at least Chase was. Not all families are as lucky when it comes to kids dealing with a gender-nonconforming sibling. We lucked out.

C.J. absolutely could not have gotten a better big brother. We remind them constantly that they are the very best of brothers. The brightest stars aligned when they were placed together.

As we try to figure out how to parent our sons—gender conforming, gender nonconforming, or other—Chase does sometimes look at us like we are from a warped universe. When we say things like "Pink is a color, and colors are for everybody!" and "Barbie is a toy, and toys are for everybody!" he sometimes, understandably, looks at us wondering how he got the weirdest family on the street. Chase has never been a rebel, but Matt and I joke that when he does go through his rebellious phase, it will include joining the Orange County Young Republicans, running off to the seminary, and living an ultraconservative lifestyle. My son's rebellious phase may remind you of Alex P. Keaton from *Family Ties*.

Because he's growing up with a gender-nonconforming brother, I've seen Chase have to deal with some of the same stuff I had to deal with growing up with a gay brother. Teasing, questioning, some embarrassment, over-the-top antics and drag. I know what it's like to have a brother who seems to hog all of the energy, air, and eyes in the room. Every day we make sure that Chase knows that he is just as loved, important, and special as his brother. Truth is, he's just as amazing as C.J. but in a less extravagant, showy way.

Chapter 12

MY BLOG GREW LEGS just as the topic of gay and gender-nonconforming youth became a cultural phenomenon. Author Cheryl Kilodavis wrote the children's book *My Princess Boy* about her son who prefers to wear dresses. J.Crew printed an ad featuring one of its executives painting her son's toenails pink and the result will forever be known as "Toemaggedon." Had there always been gender-nonconforming kids among us? Were they a new thing? Were we witnessing the feminization of boys or the deterioration of the kind of militant parenting that is hell-bent on enforcing gender and sexuality "norms" and keeping kids shamefully scared straight? People could argue both sides for days.

I believe that gender-nonconforming kids have always existed. They have to have. Come on. But the kind of parenting we've adopted, the "I'm here to love him, not change him" parenting, is new to a lot of people. I think that previous generations of gender-nonconforming kids were in hiding, some from themselves, some from their parents, some from society.

Whatever the answer, something was happening, and I had tapped into it and given it a voice. My brother had been right;

I wasn't the only parent raising a gender-nonconforming child and looking to connect with others online. That first year, I posted to my blog twice a week. Soon my posts were syndicated on Queerty.com, one of the leading websites for LGBTQ news. Readers from all walks of life tuned in. Gender-studies students and faculty at more than thirty-five colleges and universities in the U.S., the UK, and Canada asked for more; the media came calling; and blog readers started sending me research, links to articles, and videos they thought I'd find interesting. I had to set up a post-office box for C.J., who started receiving fan mail, stickers, cards, photos, toys, and clothes.

A dialogue started that now spans more than 180 countries, and as it happened, I realized something I had never thought about before: all over the world there are families raising gender-nonconforming kids. This is a global issue, one that crosses continents and cultures. I was in touch with families raising kids like C.J. all over the world: Australia, Dubai, Ireland, Africa, and the Philippines. The next generation of the LGBTQ community is being raised right now. And you know us parents, the ones raising that next generation? We have no idea what we're doing. We just want to know that we are not alone, find some comfort and camaraderie, and have someone tell us that we aren't failing.

Dr. Phil told me that I was failing. He's one of the most well-known mental-health professionals in the world, has his own daytime talk show, and was a protégé of Oprah's. Right after I started the blog and while we were choosing to accept and love our child and give him the best life possible, learning from our own past mistakes as well as others', Dr. Phil came out with startling advice on parenting a boy who likes to play with girl toys and wear girl clothes. It's simple: don't let him.

"Direct your son in an unconfusing way. Don't buy him Barbie dolls or girls' clothes. You don't want to do things that seem to support the confusion at this stage of the game. Take the girl things away, and buy him boy toys. Most importantly, support him in what he's doing, but not in the girl things," Dr. Phil said.

After reading that, I wanted to scream and cry and become defensive and find comfort in ice cream. At one point I had really thought that Dr. Phil knew his shit. When I was on maternity leave with Chase, I watched his show every day while breastfeeding as Chase and I faded in and out of a milk coma together.

Direct my son in an unconfusing way and don't buy him Barbie dolls or girls' clothes? If I took away all of C.J.'s girl toys, he would be nothing but confused. Children are not simpletons. C.J. would be confused as to why Mommy and Daddy wouldn't let him play with the things he loves to play with most. He would be confused as to why he couldn't play with girl toys but girls can play with boy toys. He would be confused as to why Chase got to select his own toys but he did not.

To me it's like saying, "What you like is not okay." And that is not okay.

C.J. would have every right to be confused and frustrated. I imagine that it would be like telling me that I should and could only enjoy hobbies and things I hate. I could go to the Supercross but not the spa. Go to the auto parts store but not the mall. Study cage fighting but not fashion magazines. Drink beer but not martinis.

Furthermore, besides feelings of confusion, C.J. might experience feelings of rejection, abuse of power, extreme jealousy, and inadequacy. I'm not willing to subject my son, either one, ever, to those feelings.

"You don't want to do things that seem to support the confusion at this stage of the game. Take the girl things away, and buy him boy toys."

I don't even want to imagine what my child would think or feel if I took away all of his "girl toys." That would leave him with his brother's old Thomas the Tank Engine trains, a Nerf gun, a plastic cowboy-and-Indian set that Pa and Nana Grab Bags brought back from a trip to Dallas, and a few other odds and ends that he has no passion for. He plays with none of these toys, but I keep them in his room, mixed in with his girl toys, in case the mood to play with boy toys ever strikes. It hasn't.

Also, I'd like to know if Dr. Phil gives the same advice to parents with little girls who want to play with cars, balls, and superhero action figures. Would he tell a tomboy's parents that their daughter might grow up to be too strong, too tough, too independent, too masculine, too "not normal," and "not okay"?

Imaginative play is encouraged in our house. No matter the character, no matter the gender.

"Most importantly, support him in what he's doing, but not in the girl things."

So I should only support a small portion of my child, since his behaviors don't fall within the range of gender normative.

I could support all of him if he were more in line with what society thinks he should be, not what he thinks he should be. I should listen to strangers, not my son. I should support Chase because he is into "boy stuff." But I shouldn't support C.J. completely because he likes "girl stuff." Support him, but only halfway. Let him know that only certain parts of him are okay. To me, that is Dr. Phil's worst suggestion of the bunch. We all deserve to be celebrated all the way.

The *Today* show discussed Dr. Phil's opinion that boys should not play with girl toys. While hosts Kathie Lee and Hoda disagreed with Dr. Phil, not all of their viewers did. Their poll question of the day was "Is it okay for boys to play with Barbies?" Only 63 percent of their voters said yes. I understand that that is still a majority, but that means 37 percent of voters didn't feel that it was permissible for a boy to play with a Barbie.

Some of the voters left comments:

Baby dolls, absolutely. Barbie dolls? Redirect to something that doesn't scream drag queen.
  —Baba

If by playing you mean ripping his sister's barbies to shreds with tools he stole from dad's workshed, sure. Redirection is in order for this situation. Get out the rescue hero guys or the lincoln logs for him to build barbie a summer home.
  —Nate

Definitely NOT!!!!!!! that's why [there are] so many FREAKS in the world now . . . boys shouldn't play with any Female dolls . . . ok nothing wrong with GI Joe cause they don't have hair 1st of all and they are skinny lil men. Barbie [has] female parts and have hair and make up.

—Monique

There is too much "feminism of America" and I admire my husband for his masculinity . . . boys should be "taught" masculinity!

—Jan

For goodness sake let children be children. If they play with Barbie or GI Joe does it really matter?

—Karen

If you try to suppress your child's interests @ a young age, you may be doing harm for them in the future. Absolutely! Gender is a social construct and there is no reason to limit our children's expressions and creativity.

—Jenn

People who say no are just being homophobic.

—Rob

The idea that toys are gender specific is outdated and offensive. Instead of teaching compliance we should be focusing on acceptance.

—Beth

I found it interesting that so many replies to this question were wallowing in veiled fear of homosexuality. I teach nursery school, and find that . . . most children don't have a problem until someone else slaps a label of "wrong" on what they're doing. In general, play is a major vehicle for a child to discover his world, and they have a heck of a good time exploring it all. A boy can learn so many positive things by playing with a doll. Gentleness, protectiveness, aspects of caregiving and responsibility for a "little" person. These things don't make him Gay, they make him a potentially good member of an adult society.

—E.S.

Dr. Phil and about half of the *Today* show's commenters infuriated me. They reminded me that a huge percentage of the population thinks that my son's gender nonconformity needs fixing, at best, and makes him an absolute freak, at worst. I can hide these people from my son when he is young, and vice versa. But as he grows, I won't be able to do that. I'll release him into a society where a lot of people will think harsh, hateful, dismissive, and dangerous thoughts about him. Thoughts that I'd hope adults would know better than to have—especially a highly visible mental-health professional like Dr. Phil.

Chapter 13

I'M ALWAYS SURPRISED BY THE HATE, intolerance, igno-
rance, and phobia that people will spew online for all to see
when they feel protected by the veil of anonymity the Internet
readily provides. It's scary when those kinds of people start to
feel brave.

A few gross people who read my blog sent e-mails informing me that C.J. would grow up to become a dick-sucking fag-
got and a "bottom" who liked to be dominated by a "top"
because he would have "mommy and daddy issues."

> Social Services should take your child away, you are en-
> couraging him to have a paraphillia [*sic*].
> I'm calling them right now to tell you you are forcing
> him to wear girls clothing and making him play with dolls all
> because of your agenda. Every objective person could see
> it's not [the] child who wants the dolls, it's you who wants
> your child to want dolls.
> Sad and pathetic.
> There's nothing wrong with a kid being gay and liking

dolls, but is something wrong with forcing it upon him, you terrible mother.

—Joe

CJ's mom, if your child wanted to kill your pets would you be so happy about it? Or if your child got really happy trying to jump off a ladder or wanted to drive your car would you allow him to do this?

For God sakes you so called mothers what the hell have you been brought up on. This is your child yet you have given up on them without even trying. This is so wrong. If you do not believe in the Bible then I guess there's nothing to talk about but if you do, believe for your child because this is not what God intended for him. There are way too many scriptures that say this is wrong but it will be you who will have to stand before God about this. If the Bible said that being gay was okay, then I would be okay with it too but woman this is just wrong and I truly believe one day you will regret this mistake.

—Monica

When I read some comments or e-mails, I had to remind myself that I didn't start my blog to fight or prove a point; that I shouldn't write and publish things in the heat of the moment or out of defensiveness; and that some commenters and readers are hateful and tacky and reveal themselves to be the kind of people whom I need to protect C.J. from and teach him about. Above all else, the blog has taught me to more patient than I am generally programmed to be.

I've had people accuse me of desperately wanting my son to be gay and trying to make him that way. Loving my brother as much as I do, I have always been able to say, comfortably and confidently, that I have never *wanted* either of my sons to be gay. I realize that that statement can be taken negatively. But here's the thing. I am a mother, and I have the same primal wants for my children that every parent has: health, happiness, safety, length of life, etc.

I want my sons not to have an easy life with the best seat on the gravy train, but I'd like the challenges that they encounter in life to be fair, surmountable, and just frequent enough to make them strong, courageous, intelligent men. I don't wish for them to have to endure unnecessary hardships in life. I don't wish for them to suffer from prejudices against them that are based on things out of their control.

I want them to be great people with enough competitive spirit and self-confidence to drive them to follow and excel at their passions—be those styling hair, serving their country, performing, or driving trash trucks. I want them to have just enough competitive spirit and self-confidence, but not so much that they risk meaningful relationships and become consumed by their own self-righteousness. I don't ever want them to feel like true fulfillment is unattainable.

I want them to fall in love with their whole heart, more than once. I want them to have a significant other in their life who fills them, completes them, and isn't chosen out of compromise, ambivalence, or apathy. I want them to have someone whom they want to care for and who wants to care for them.

I want them to have a moral compass that works better than

my own. I want them to know right from wrong, to consider other people's feelings and the consequences of their actions. I want them to be men who do the right thing simply because it is the right thing to do.

These are the wants I have for my sons. I don't want them to be gay. I am not raising them with any great hopes that they will love men and we will be unique and I can feel trendy flaunting their sexuality.

If they are gay, I have all of the same wants for them. I may be sad, realizing that they will have to endure hardships, struggles, judgments, and taunts that they haven't earned but that will be forced on them simply because of whom they were created to love. I may cry in private. I may worry more excessively. I may feel that they have been dealt a fate that is not always just or right.

More than that, I will fight for them with a love and loyalty that is so strong it will never be broken. I will support them and their partners and their rights as if they were my own.

Decades from now, when someone asks about my son's wife or girlfriend, I will not be ashamed or engulfed by a moment's hesitation when informing the person that there is no wife or girlfriend or female in the world who would make him nearly as happy as his fabulous same-sex partner.

I want my sons to know a world and a life that allows them to walk in the sun, follow their fancies, and explore unhindered by the phobias of any group. I don't want them to ever feel small. I want them to be responsible, successful, competent, smart, confident, caring men. No mother would wish extra and unjustified hardships on her children. We try to fix what is broken, and to so many in this cruel world being a member of the LGBTQ community is to be broken.

I'm not trying to change either of my sons into something that he is not. Quite the opposite. I'm trying to celebrate and support them so they know that they are free to be exactly who they were created to be.

Chapter 14

IN FEBRUARY, AS WE BEGAN planning for C.J.'s fourth birthday, with the prior year's Disney Princess birthday cake and voyeuristic partygoers in mind, we ran some ideas by him. He wanted Disney Princess party supplies, an *Alice in Wonderland* cake, a Barbie bounce house, and only guacamole to eat. A multithemed pink-and-purple fiesta.

"Hey, C.J., what if this year for your birthday we went to Disneyland to meet all of the princesses and Alice?" (If you ask me, it's a shame that poor Alice was never initiated into the Disney Princess gang, because she has real moxie.) "We could ride on rides all day, visit the Princess Fantasy Faire, see Mickey's and Minnie's houses"—he was surprised they didn't live together, he's so progressive—"have lunch at Snow White's restaurant, and you can pick out birthday presents at one of the many overpriced souvenir shops. What would you think about that?" Matt and I said, hoping that he would like our proposition.

We didn't want to opt out of a party; we just wanted to opt in to something more perfect. We wanted a celebration that didn't revisit the awkward moments and apprehension of the party from the year before. There were no words to express C.J.'s great joy, but there were screams of delight and a dance that included sticking his tongue out while thrusting his hips back and forth while using big jazz hands.

"You can have a birthday party in the backyard instead, if you want," we offered again.

"NO! I wanna go to Disneyland and see my princesses," he insisted.

Part of me felt like we were swindling him out of a birthday party just because we were being overprotective and were afraid that he might get teased or judged negatively if we had the obligatory Orange County fourth-birthday-party spectacle for our boy, who would, no doubt, select a total and complete "girl theme." For weeks I asked him if he'd rather have a birthday party or go to Disneyland. The choice was his, and the answer was Disneyland every time.

I called Disneyland to book a birthday lunch with the princesses at Ariel's Grotto. They assumed we were celebrating the birthday of my daughter.

"No, it's for my son," I said.

The sweet Disney cast member was unfazed.

"Do you have very many boys who want to celebrate their birthday with the princesses?" I digressed.

"It's not uncommon," she said.

We're not uncommon, I told myself. *We're not uncommon!*

We woke up early on C.J.'s birthday, drove to Disneyland, parked our car, walked to the tram, rode the tram, and walked to the entrance. Finally, all that was standing between the mouse and us was security.

"What? Does he play with Barbies?" asked a security

woman I will refer to as Virginia Slims, in large part because of her gravelly voice and the telltale smoker's wrinkles that ringed her mouth. She was eyeing the doll in my son's hands.

"Yeah, he does," I said as I opened our backpack for inspection.

"Really? He plays with Barbies?" Virginia Slims asked again, more interested in my response than in whether I had large amounts of explosives in my bag.

"Yes. He. Does," I said with a psychotic smile spreading across my face, eyes frozen and teeth clenched in fake politeness.

"Well, I guess that's all right," she said, shrugging her shoulders. Well, thank you, oh wise bag checker at Disneyland, for letting me know that it is okay for my son to play with Barbies. I had been wondering from whom I should seek affirmation. And besides, it wasn't just a Barbie; it was Disney's Rapunzel. So there.

The rest of the day was pure Disney magic.

We headed straight for Fantasyland for the *Alice in Wonderland* ride because C.J. wanted to ride a "pat-a-pillar" (caterpillar, for those who don't speak four-year-old) and fall down the "rabbit ho" (hole, for those with their minds in the gutter). We rode ride after ride after ride.

Then we hit the high note of our day: the Disney Princess Fantasy Faire. After all, C.J. had wanted to visit Disneyland to see *his* princesses. I had read on Disneyland's website as I planned our day:

Meet some of your favorite Disney Princesses in person at Disney Princess Fantasy Faire. Walk down an enchanting pathway with scenic alcoves perfect for introducing little ones to each princess. Be sure to take a picture and make the special moment last forever! You never know which Disney Princesses will drop by Disney Princess Fantasy Faire to say hello. The greeting pathway usually features 3 Disney Princesses at any given time.

Oh, we did it; we walked the enchanting pathway and visited the scenic alcoves. We got to meet Snow White, Aurora (a.k.a. Sleeping Beauty), and Jasmine.

I told Snow White, the first princess on our route, that it was C.J.'s birthday and all he wanted was to meet the princesses. She gave him the royal treatment, and each princess escorted us and personally introduced C.J. to the next. It was the happiest ten minutes of his short life. When C.J. gets nervous he stands up really straight, puts both hands behind his back, and wrings and twiddles his fingers like he's trying to pull them off. They were in full motion at the Fantasy Faire.

We conveniently exited into an all-princess gift shop, and C.J. picked out his favorite present since Christmas's Disney's *Tangled* Rapunzel Braiding Friends Hair Braider.

It was a plush doll. Hold her one way and she is Aurora; flip her over and her dress cascades down, covering her up and revealing Ariel, who was under Aurora's skirt. (How Ariel got under there and what she was doing is none of my business.)

The day at Disneyland had initially been conjured up to protect our family and felt like a second-choice option. By the end of our day, it felt like the best decision we had made in months. And it's still one of our favorite days that we've had as a family. It wasn't what was expected; it wasn't a huge birthday party to which everyone we knew (or didn't know) was invited. C.J. has taught us that "the expected" and "the normal" aren't always what they are cracked up to be. He's taught us to question those concepts, and when we do, we get a different perspective that we are thankful to have. It's a perspective that we might not have if we didn't have C.J.

Chapter 15

AT C.J.'S FOUR-YEAR CHECKUP with his pediatrician (you know, the one I had test him for color blindness), I explained that I believed C.J. was gender nonconforming. The pediatrician looked a little bewildered and referred us to the department of psychiatry, where we got an appointment a few weeks later with a child psychiatrist. Did I think that C.J. needed mental-health help at that point? No. But I was eager to talk to anybody who might have experience with or information about gender-nonconforming kids.

We arrived at our appointment with the assigned basic intake forms filled out. Is your child depressed? No. Has your child tried to harm himself or others? No. He just likes to play with Barbies and cross-dress. There was no question about that.

We walked into the psychiatrist's office, and C.J. made a beeline for the toy castle in the corner. He cleared all of the knights out and gathered the princesses for play. The 'fro-headed white doctor in a Tommy Bahama shirt observed him. We observed the doctor observing him.

"Oh, there is one other form I need you to fill out," the

doctor said, handing me three sheets of paper with questions printed on the front and back.

Across the top of the first page it read, "Test for Sexual Deviancy."

"It's standard in cases like these," the doctor assured me after, I'm sure, I made some sort of face while reading the title.

"Does your child masturbate him/her self?" No.

"Has your child tried to masturbate someone other than him/her self?" God, no!

"Has you child experienced penile discharge? If so, does he play with it or his feces?" Oh, hell no!

"Has your child attempted sex with an animal?"

"I'm not answering this. This isn't our son," I said, handing the papers back to the doctor, waving them in the air between us, signaling that I wanted to be rid of them as quickly as possible.

Matt grabbed the papers from me, thinking I was being defiant when maybe I should be being compliant. His eyes grew big and his face grew red as he scanned the questions.

"No, that's not our son," he said sternly, pushing the papers back toward the doctor.

From there, things in the tiny psychiatry office grew awkward and very, very quiet as all eyes went to C.J., not wanting to go anywhere else.

"What?" C.J. said, noticing that we were all watching him.

"Nothing, baby," I said. We all smiled. I was fighting back tears.

As our appointment was nearing an end, the doctor looked through one of his magic books and then confirmed what I had already learned online. C.J. was gender nonconforming.

The doctor told us that C.J. had no need for continuing treatment and gave us some generic parenting handouts, which I threw in the trash as we exited the building.

"At least we know that our son isn't a sexual deviant. How many parents can say that about their four-year-old?" I said to Matt. He had no comment.

As Matt drove home, I was deep in thought. I thought about the appointment, the child psychiatrist, and the sexual-deviancy test. I decided that I would become the expert on our son; we wouldn't look to anybody else to fill that role in the future. I felt like a professional researcher for the better part of a year. It got obnoxious. I'd never been so fact hungry in my life, except for when Jackie Kennedy Onassis died and in the months leading up to Prince William and Kate Middleton's nuptials.

One month later I was at the park watching a friend of C.J.'s run around pretending to be Super Mario while C.J. was giving a rousing rendition of Princess Peach.

I was sitting on a bench completely engrossed in an article from *Parenting* magazine titled "Could Your Child Be Gay?" All of a sudden this stealthy neighborhood dad was sitting right next to me on the bench, smiling. He was like a phantom who had caught me rainbow handed. I fumbled with my papers. My hands were out of my control. I flipped over the article as quickly as I could and hid it beneath my purse. I felt like a sixteen-year-old boy caught with porn. I really didn't need anybody sneaking a peek at the title of the article I was reading. What would they think? Once the dad left to push his son on a swing, I continued reading.

"Besides an affinity for pink and for playing dress-up (for

boys), there are certain other behaviors that might raise a parent's brow: children who often pretend to be the opposite sex, or who prefer to play only with them; a passion (for a girl) or a dislike (for a boy) of rough play; or a preference for dressing like the opposite sex in everyday situations as opposed to isolated incidents. The official psychological term for these types of behaviors is 'gender nonconformity,' " the article read.

"No matter how you or your spouse feels about it, one thing is certain for all kids: Children are desperate to know that they're loved and accepted by their parents. You need to make the decision that your child's happiness and safety is totally unrelated to his sexual orientation. . . . The one place kids cannot be afraid is in their homes," said Judy Shepard, cofounder of the Matthew Shepard Foundation.

"New research in the *Journal of Pediatrics* suggests that gay, lesbian and bisexual young adults from very rejecting families (as opposed to families who were neutral or mildly rejecting) are nearly six times more likely to have major depression and three to five times more likely to use illegal drugs or have unprotected sex," the article reported.

I finished the article and wondered what the chances were that some other adult at the park was reading the same article and wondering if, in fact, their child could be gay. A woman was on her cell phone. A grandfather was eating an ice cream. That neighborhood dad continued to push his son on a swing. I rounded up Super Mario and Princess Peach and we headed for the car. I had a little squishy hand in each of mine. Could C.J. be gay? Could he be straight? Could he be transgender?

"I love you no matter what," I told him.

"I know," he said with a smile.

In my online research, I found horrible examples of families who tried to force their little gender-nonconforming sons to conform, families who didn't love their child no matter what. Anderson Cooper did a report titled "The Sissy Boy Experiment," about experimental therapy conducted on a five-year-old boy named "Kraig" in the 1970s at UCLA in an attempt to make him less effeminate and prevent him from growing into a gay adult. As part of the therapy, his mother would reward him for masculine behavior and his father would beat him for feminine behavior. The study was government funded and considered to be a great success, even though the family says that it was disastrous and the boy grew up to be gay and ultimately committed suicide.

The story made my heart break. Snapped it right into tiny pieces. That would teach me to watch CNN instead of E!

I Googled "The Sissy Boy Experiment" and read an article in *Time* reporting that "some of the most harrowing cases of psychological and medical malpractice involve attempts to change a child's gender or sexual identity. Not only have such misguided 'therapies' often resulted in patients' suicides, but they also repeatedly appear to foster scientific misconduct."

I made up my own serenity prayer while out jogging the next day. *God, grant me the serenity to be an awesome mom for my gender-nonconforming child and the courage not to send him to UCLA to be experimented on; and wisdom, because we are different. Oh, and watch over Anderson Cooper, too. Amen.*

Chapter 16

IT'S NOT ALWAYS EASY FOR C.J. to find peers with whom he connects, peers who accept him and realize how truly fabulous he is. Friendships from his toddler years haven't all lasted. Once his former best friend (a gender-conforming boy) took up *Star Wars* and C.J. started running with princesses, they slowly went their separate ways. But there are the tried-and-true friends he's had since birth and there are the new kids he's met along the rainbow way. These are special friendships with special kids who are bored by traditional gender roles and so much more fond of being fluid. And if a girl already has her first GBF (gay best friend) at age four, she's light-years ahead of the rest of the female population, who go in search of their GBF in college. And when C.J. does connect with a friend on a real level? Hold on to your tiaras, because something magical happens.

Two little boys were at a park in South Orange County. One was five years old, the other four. Both had Strawberry Shortcake in one hand, facing each other so that Ms. Shortcake could have a word with her clone. Both boys had a hand on the right hip, head cocked to the right, with total attitude.

They were deep in play. I couldn't tell what was transpiring between the two Strawberry Shortcakes, but I could tell that my son was in heaven, even though he was acting like a total diva. I was pretty much inside the pearly gates too, because it was the first time my son had ever played with a little boy so much like him.

John's mom, Jennifer, had found my blog and e-mailed me. I'm so thankful that she found me and insisted that we meet and get the boys together to play. She was right: our lives were uncannily similar. C.J. met John on a "blind playdate" arranged by us meddling mothers, who had wrongly assumed that they would never find another girly boy to play with.

John likes the "girl toy" with his Happy Meal at McDonald's, loves the Disney Princesses, and likes to slip into his Mary Janes after a long day at school. John walked up to us at the park hiding a stuffed-animal kitty behind his back. He saw C.J.'s plush Rapunzel doll in full view, and his kitty quickly came out to play.

John is marvelous. He's a bespectacled, long-lashed, tender soul with a mop of long, sandy brown hair. He wears the same shoes, but in different colors. He's a magnet for wonder.

Jennifer is equally cool. She rocks worn cowboy boots and a cardigan with eclectic brooches that John plays with when he's feeling a little shy. She serves organic strawberries and is dead set, like me, on not changing her little boy, just loving him.

John and C.J. both have older brothers who are all boy and dads who, though they may struggle from time to time, love them completely and now know the difference between a Bratz doll, a Barbie, and an American Girl.

John and C.J. played Strawberry Shortcake and Rapunzel, nibbled on Disney Princess fruit snacks, and went on a discovery hike to look for ladybugs. They were oblivious to looks from other parkgoers.

Jennifer and I sat on a bench and talked. What are your feelings about your son wearing something girly outside of the house? What do you do when your son wants to have a Pinkalicious-themed birthday party? Why is the Rapunzel dress at the Disney Store fifty dollars?!

We both struggle to protect our sons while also trying to set them free. We have to get creative when it comes to birthday parties, judgmental friends, and dressing our feminine boys.

She had tips for me because she was a year further along in the adventures of raising a gender-nonconforming son. She also had warnings. C.J. may start to get embarrassed and withdrawn in the coming year because he may begin to realize that he is different. Some of his innocence may fly away as the reality of life crawls in. I listened and took mental notes.

John had had show-and-tell that morning at school. It took him some time to decide what to take to share with the class. He weighed his options. Take a "girl toy" he loved and possibly get made fun of or take a "boy toy" he wasn't as excited about and not get made fun of? He played it safe. He took a brown teddy bear. No one made fun of him, and he was happy.

That's another thing Jennifer and I talked about: how at ages four and five our sons make a lot of decisions based on whether or not they will be teased. We both feel that our kids are too young to have to know how to make decisions based on the outcome. Other kids their ages don't have to weigh those options. It's not fair, but it has also developed their thought processes. So we take the silver lining.

Our first two hours together felt like ten minutes, and we lost track of time. We gathered our things and our sons in a hurried panic. We didn't want to be late to pick up the older brothers from school. Jennifer e-mailed me later that night to let me know that, as they drove away from our playdate, John said, "Mom, I can't believe C.J. likes princesses! That is so great that he won't even make fun of me!"

John's comment made every part of me happy and sad all at the same time. I was happy that the boys had found a gender-nonconforming friend whom they could truly be their whole selves around and sad that they had endured teasing before finding such a friend.

On our next playdate C.J. and I ventured to John's house by the beach, where I could smell the ocean from the backyard. It was the perfect place to sip iced tea and chat it up with my new mom friend. C.J. loved it because John's dress-up collection could make even a gender-conforming boy want to dress up like a girl. Even better, it was on a small rolling garment rack. C.J. pushed it as if he were rolling a new collection to Lincoln Center during New York's Fashion Week. He watched the clothes sway as he moved the rack.

"Where did you get a kid-sized garment rack?" I asked Jennifer. I wanted one.

"Believe it or not, I got it at Walmart. The boxes of dress-up clothes were overflowing and driving me crazy. I needed to bring some order to his dresses," she said.

"I need to get C.J. one of those for his dresses."

C.J. rolled the rack back to its parking spot. The boys put on dresses and headed for the trampoline. C.J. was wearing a Rapunzel dress and John was wearing a long black velvet dress.

"See! That's the Rapunzel dress from the Disney Store. It was fifty dollars! I don't even spend that much money on a dress for myself!" Jennifer said. "He got it for his birthday."

"I know! They have one at Walmart, but it's not made as well. I'm going to see if the costume store has one on sale after Halloween. He wants that particular gown so bad," I said.

A conversation only moms of gender-nonconforming sons could have.

After lunch Jennifer made play dough with the boys.

"What color do you want to make it?" she asked, showing them all of her food colorings.

"Purple!" John shouted.

"Pink!" C.J. cheered.

"Pink and purple it is!" Jennifer said.

John's brother joined us after he got home from school. He was a ball of gender-conforming boyness and reminded me of Chase. He licked an ice cream as he watched C.J. and John make pink and purple play dough while wearing dresses. He observed and smiled. I knew it was good for him to see that there were other boys out there like his brother.

Jennifer and I both wished that John and C.J. could go through school together, because there is safety in numbers and because then neither one would ever feel like the odd boy out.

At the time, in C.J.'s preschool class there were about a dozen boys and one girl. Guess who was C.J.'s BFF? The one little girl, whom he affectionately called Cookie, because her real name was too hard for him to say. It was Cookie plus C.J. sitting in a tree.

"When you had your parent-teacher conference, did Ms. Kyna talk to you about our kids needing to keep their hands to themselves and them being too touchy-feely with each other?" Cookie's mom asked Matt one day as they picked the kids up from school. Ms. Kyna hadn't brought the issue to our attention.

"Do you and Cookie touch each other at school?" we asked C.J. later that night, trying to seem very casual about the whole thing.

"Yeah," he said nonchalantly.

"What do you mean?" we asked, meeting him on the corner of casual and nonchalant.

"We hold hands and hug each udder," he said.

"Do you kiss?" My question earned a wide-eyed look from Matt.

"Gross! Yeah, sometimes. Cookie asks me to kiss her on the cheek 'cause we's gonna get married," C.J. explained.

I thought about how Cookie might be a good match for C.J. Or she might make gender even more fluid for him. Cookie was a cutie with short brown curly hair, sleepy eyes, and a bright smile. She wore old-school red Chucks and *Toy Story* shirts and carried a Batman backpack filled with her dinosaur toys. She liked all superheroes, but Spider-Man and Iron Man were her absolute favorites. Cookie was very territorial—I mean protective—of C.J. Even her twin sister knew to keep her hands off him. A distance of ten feet was preferred by Cookie.

Cookie and C.J. had little in common, except that they both appeared to be creative when it came to gender. They were a quirky match made on the preschool playground.

When an invite to Cookie and her sister's pirate-themed fourth birthday party made its way into C.J.'s backpack, you'd have thought he'd been invited to the Oscars.

Finally, the day of the party arrived. It was not a girly pirate theme with pink Jolly Rogers sporting heart-shaped eye patches. No, this was a legit pirate party, and dress-up was encouraged.

"C.J., we get to dress up for Cookie's pirate party. Isn't that fun?"

"Woo-hoo! I wanna be a princess," he said.

"No, Cookie wants you to dress like a pirate," I informed him.

"Tell Cookie I don't wanna be a pirate. I wanna be a princess."

"But it's Cookie's party, and she wants all of her friends to be pirates," I explained.

"When it's my berfday party, can my friends dress up how I want them?"

"Sure," I said, not wanting to argue.

Cripes almighty, that was a big promise that I hoped he would forget about, but he probably wouldn't, and I'd have to deal with that when the time came. I'm pretty sure all of the boys and dads wouldn't want to attend C.J.'s next birthday party dressed as princesses or cheerleaders. Although that would be fun for my girlfriends and me to see.

I loaded my pirate into the car.

Burgers. Bounce house. Bubbles. Then, face painting. The

birthday girls got to be first, naturally. Cookie's sister wanted to be Captain America, while Cookie chose Spider-Man. Up next? C.J., who was painted into one fierce Wonder Woman. The three gender-creative superheroes got together for a picture.

"That's so funny, the twins wanted to be boys and the boy wanted to be a girl," I heard a grandmotherly partygoer say.

"They are quite a team," I said to Cookie's mom as we watched our three opposite-gendered superheroes.

"They sure are," she agreed.

"I like that you let the girls like whatever they want to like." It was the first time I had ever broached the subject with Cookie's mom.

"Of course, they're just kids," she said.

"Yup," I replied.

It was time for balloon animals. Cookie and her sister requested swords. C.J. wanted a pretty pink flower. While the girls waved their swords at C.J., he sniffed his aromatic pink latex daisy. The girls started chasing C.J. He shrieked and ran away, hugging his pink flower.

During gift time, Cookie unwrapped the Super Hero Squad Headquarters we bought for her, and Cookie's sister unwrapped the My Little Pony with baby pony and stroller. They both hopped up to hug C.J. in gratitude. They lingered and fought over who would release him first. Adults were laughing. I was too. When the embrace was done, C.J. turned to me in silent tears.

"What's wrong, honey?" I asked, bending down to his level.

"I want that My Little Pony."

"When it's your birthday, you can get that My Little Pony,"

I said, knowing that was a promise I could and would make good on.

After saying our good-byes, we piled into the car and my pirate Wonder Woman with the pink flower slept all the way home.

Chapter 17

C.J. AND COOKIE'S TEACHER, Ms. Kyna, is a special kind of angel who spreads goodness with construction paper, finger paints, and songs that require corresponding hand gestures. When C.J. first entered her classroom, he was three, and his gender nonconformity was emerging but largely contained by us and limited to the safety of our house. Over the course of the year and a half he spent with her, he flourished as a person, a student, and a gender nonconformist.

Ms. Kyna started to pick up on C.J.'s gender nonconformity and only hinted at it at first. Which is what people typically do once they realize that he is different.

"He is just so sweet" or "What a unique boy" or "He's a creative one, that's for sure" or "Bless his little heart" is usually what people say when they don't know what to say about C.J. I have come to feel that, when describing C.J., "sweet," "unique," and "creative" equal "girly," "different," or "gay." Ms. Kyna even went so far as to call him an "angel." That's when I knew that she knew.

"I found your blog," she said sweetly and shyly one afternoon when I was picking C.J. up from school.

"Oh, you did? What did you think?" I asked. It was the first time I had been discovered. I felt exposed and tingly. This could change everything.

She told me that she thought it was great and that she adored C.J. and our family. Our relationship turned a corner that day. I felt it happen: she was no longer just a fan of our team; she was a part of it. I began to see how much she celebrated C.J., supported him, protected him, and advocated for him. She thought that he was pretty fabulous. As C.J. approached the end of his first full year in preschool, Ms. Kyna scheduled the obligatory parent-teacher conference to discuss C.J.'s progress and educational future. Ms. Kyna, two other preschool professionals, Matt, and I were all in attendance.

The best line from Ms. Kyna's six-page evaluation of C.J.? "C.J. stands up for his rights." Matt and I were convinced that was Ms. Kyna's nice way of saying that C.J. is a total diva at school, just like he is at home. When I called her on it, she smiled and said that C.J. was her star pupil. Apparently, sometimes, Ms. Kyna skirts the truth while wearing rose-colored glasses.

At the end of the meeting, one of the preschool professionals said, "I just want to follow C.J. and know if he turns out to be a hairdresser when he grows up. Because every time I need his full attention and cooperation, I bribe him with the promise of getting to brush the hair of a princess doll that I have in class."

Everybody from the school nodded their head in agreement and smiled warm smiles. It was the first Matt and I were hearing of the bribery to brush hair that the school used as a motivator when teaching C.J. Our secret had been out of the bag. These teachers knew the way to our son's heart, and it was through princesses and pretty hair. They all seriously wanted to be kept apprised of C.J.'s path in life; they couldn't help but be curious. It was the first time we realized that C.J. does that to people: he sparks their curiosity. People who come to know him want to know what happens in his life, want to follow his journey. As if his life were a book you don't want to put down.

"I'm glad that our son stands up for his rights. That's good. He'll need that tenacity in life," I said to Matt as we walked to our car after the meeting at the preschool.

"Yeah, as long as he is respectful to the teachers and other kids and doesn't think he's running the show," Matt said.

"I'm also glad he has a thing for hair, because if he does turn out to be a hairdresser, this mama is going save a lot of money on highlights and Brazilian blowouts," I added.

"Of course you are," Matt said as we got into the car.

It felt like a gloomy day when C.J. graduated from Ms. Kyna's class. I got to thinking. Where we live, many families hold their boys back a year in school with high hopes that it will give their son an advantage and that he will excel athletically and be the star of his sports team and, with a decade or so of private coaching at a hundred dollars per hour, go on to play his sport of choice professionally. C.J. could be one of those boys, although it might not be sports he has an affinity for. Perhaps holding him back would position him to be the best glee clubber, thespian, cheer captain, designer, or stylist. Maybe I could hold him back and keep him with Ms. Kyna. During the weeks leading up to our big good-bye, I had questioned Ms. Kyna incessantly.

"Are you sure he's ready to move on?"

"Maybe one more year with you would even better prepare him for prekindergarten or kindergarten."

"Is there any way we can keep him here?"

"He's ready to move on," Ms. Kyna said, trying to reassure me. "I hate to see him go, but he's going to be fine. He's ready."

She knew that I was scared to leave the safety of her classroom. I felt like there were layers of protection that I had wrapped around my son for his own good, but in a lot of instances they were there to make Matt and me feel less vulnerable. Graduating from Ms. Kyna's preschool program was like tearing off one of those protective layers, leaving us a little more susceptible to the cruelty of the world that we had not yet seen but knew was out there.

Most mothers would be delighted and proud that their child had tested out of a certain academic program and was ready to advance. I was sad. We had been safe, and now we only had a few months of summer to prepare for the world of prekindergarten.

Chapter 18

WE SPENT OUR SUMMER trying not to stress about the up-
coming school year. We made our annual pilgrimage to the
San Juan National Forest, which is the backyard of Grandma
and Grandpa Colorado, who are also known as Matt's parents.
Driving to their house takes fourteen hours. We all go bat-
shit crazy by the time we arrive and get out of the car looking
like wide-eyed lunatics suffering from post-traumatic stress
disorder after having endured hours of torture at the hands of
the desolate Indian reservations we have to drive through and
the processed food we eat to keep ourselves busy. The kids are
forever traumatized by stopping at no less than five gas-station
restrooms and trying to go to the bathroom while I yell repeatedly, "Don't. Touch. Anything!" Sometimes a mother
feels like there isn't enough hand sanitizer in the world.

A few days into our two-week stay, we were sitting on the
deck enjoying the evening quiet before dinner. We were com-
menting that out in nature you can actually hear the wind as it
brushes past trees. You don't hear the wind in suburbia.

"Daddy, I like boy stuff when I'm in Colorado," C.J. said
out of the blue.

Matt whipped his head in my direction. I knew what he was thinking. We were both doing the math. We could sell our home in Orange County and buy a nice home on a few acres in Colorado with cash. What would we do for work? How are the schools? How are the winters? Would my new wardrobe be rustic vintage cowgirl or bohemian cowgirl chic?

Then I flashed forward ten years and knew for certain that if C.J. continued to be gender nonconforming, this small town would be the absolute worst place to raise him. The population of fifteen hundred is mostly Ute Indians or white, unemployed single people living below the poverty line. The local economy is saved by the retirees who, during the months of the year that they reside locally, volunteer, donate, and do good.

I've heard of families who move from, say, California to Washington because skin cancer runs in their family and they want to save their children from the disease so they flee the sun. I wondered: if relocating from California to Colorado would change our gender-nonconforming son into a gender-conforming one, would we move? At that time we really considered it.

If moving halfway across the country would save one or all members of our family from unnecessary hardships, would we—should we—move? Can you outrun gender nonconformity? If moving would make our family "normal," would we do it? Did we want to be normal? Would a move to Colorado be well intentioned for the sake of our son or a desperate attempt to change him? I asked myself a lot of questions.

C.J.'s gender identity, his perception of gender, and his unique gender presentation are a part of him; they go where he goes. We could take the gender-nonconforming boy out of California, but we couldn't take the gender nonconformity out of the boy. Five days earlier, we were at home and C.J. wanted to pack his hand-me-down pink flower-girl dress, tap shoes, and brown lip gloss for his trip to the wilderness.

This town is tiny in population but huge in backwardness. And its residents obviously take consumerism lightly. The nearest escalator is an hour and a half away. There is no big-box store, as they call them. No Target, no Walmart, no Kmart, no Costco. They recently got a Sonic fast-food restaurant but boycott it in favor of the local malt shop, which is named, cleverly, the Malt Shoppe. There are no paid firefighters; they're all volunteers. Should a blaze be set, the town would be screwed. The local police officer lives down the street. If his car is in his driveway, it's a good time to commit a crime.

Then I got to thinking. Even I like boy stuff more in Colorado. I ride ATVs, I shoot guns, I zip-line, I hold a pole and pretend to fish, and I even had a sip of beer. I'm gender nonconforming in Colorado. Put that on a T-shirt and I'll wear it to the local PFLAG meeting. What's that? Their local PFLAG chapter has been inactive for years because it only had one member? Damn.

Added to all of that, Grandma Colorado has only "boy toys" at her house because that's all there is in the family, all that there has been for decades. Boys, lots of them. And then along came C.J. to a family and a piece of the state where the men are manly and so are the women.

My best friend's husband, Sullivan, joined us for a few days in Colorado that year. He was there when C.J. cried as we removed him from an ATV. He wanted "more motorcycle rides." Sullivan looked at me and amusedly said, "Uh-oh. What are you gonna do? What are you going to blog about now?"

Was my little rainbow turning all blue?

Not so fast. As it turned out, while the rest of the family was making the NRA proud and shooting guns after lunch, C.J. refused to wear ear protectors until he saw that one pair had a pink sticker on it. He claimed that pair real quick. At night we were covered in filth. C.J. eyed Grandma's pink soap rose petals and candles and had a bath by candlelight with floating pink petals nightly. Grandma has two sets of silverware, one more modern and one older, with lots of scrolls and roses. C.J. would eat only with the frilly ones, because "they are the ones the princesses use."

I remembered back to the previous summer, when we had been in Colorado with a three-year-old C.J. and Michael and his boyfriend house-sat for us—which really means that they wanted to sit poolside, use our air-conditioning, and drink our liquor. I called them halfway through the trip and gave them a mission. They were expressly instructed to hide all of C.J.'s girl stuff.

Michael did as he was told because he was staying in our house with free room and board for a week and because, as much as he is comfortable with his LGBTQ lifestyle, he knows that conforming to a certain extent would protect C.J. We had all continued to wonder, if all of the girl stuff were gone, would C.J. learn to like only boy stuff?

C.J. didn't asked for his girl toys when we got home. Outta sight, outta mind. Instead, he had played with all of the girl toys that were left out, because Michael and his boyfriend had apparently done a shitty of job of the simple task of identifying a "girl toy," putting it in a bag, and putting the bag in my closet.

"You missed at least two Barbies, a Tinker Bell, and a Strawberry Shortcake!" I informed my brother over the phone.

"I'm sorry, I just wasn't good at that job. I didn't see them," he said.

We had all been getting so used to girl toys that we didn't even notice them; they weren't sticking out as much. I remember the days when one doll stuck out like a sore thumb in our house. Michael and his boyfriend really had tried, they'd sworn.

Once we got home from the trip, the weeks passed and I'd slowly reintroduced some of the hidden contraband back into C.J.'s life on the sly, mingling them in with all of the girl toys Michael and his boyfriend left out. It was cheaper than buying new toys, and I'd felt guilty. There's nothing like a mother's guilt. Some of the toys I'd thrown away because they were old and overused anyway.

In a flash of stupidity, it crossed my mind to do the same thing again this year, to have the girl stuff gone when we arrived home from Colorado. But I had learned my lesson and resisted the urge. C.J. could like girl stuff in California and boy stuff in Colorado. He can like whatever he wants in whatever state he wants. I'm just glad that he gets the opportunity to be exposed to it all. That's what I want for my kids, to be exposed to lots of different things and choose their own passions, not mine or anybody else's. No more suffocating dolls in the back of a dark closet at home.

Chapter 19

WE SEE GRANDMA AND GRANDPA Colorado only a few times each year, which would be totally fine if I didn't like them so much. How I managed to luck out in the in-law department is beyond me, and it's not that we have so much in common. My mother-in-law is a total tomboy. She was a professional surfer. She hates to shop. She couldn't care less about celebrity gossip, mostly because she is unfamiliar with most celebrities. She recently went three years without a television. I told her that Michael Jackson had died six months after his death, and she was shocked, though not sad. She doesn't know her way around a computer or the mall. She doesn't care about things like matching her clothes, climbing the corporate ladder, or preventative maintenance. She amuses me to no end.

My father-in-law might have been my soul mate had I been born thirty years earlier. He's a dichotomy. He's a man's man with a master's degree in English and a hankering for whiskey. He knows every pre-Y2K song that comes on the radio and will dance to the song with a grace not known to many men over six feet. He collects quotes and knives. He has an artist's spirit with a blue-collar sensibility. He understands women, fish, and woodworking better than any person I've ever met. He calls me and my friends sexist nicknames like Baby Doll, Baby Girl, and Filly, not only are we not bothered by it, but we kind of like it.

Grandma and Grandpa Colorado are children of the sixties. They met in Manhattan Beach, got married months later, and joined the Peace Corps, but they're not the hippies you might believe them to be. They are old-fashioned and traditional in many, many ways.

They've always welcomed my gay brother into their lives and home with big, burly arms. But he's not their son, so it's a little easier to be accepting and loving and then send him back home on the evening train to West Hollywood. C.J. is different; he's their flesh and blood. I used to wonder if they attributed C.J.'s being gender nonconforming to me. As far as we know, they've never had an LGBTQ person in their bloodline, so I'm sure they think that he can't possibly be their fault.

"I just can't believe that Matt is so forgiving of C.J.," Grandma Colorado said to me during our trip to Colorado as she sipped the mojito I had just introduced her to.

"What do you mean?" I asked.

"I can't believe that Matt is so forgiving of C.J. . . . and you, I guess. Because your brother is gay and C.J. is the way he is," she said.

"Do you mean 'forgiving' or 'accepting'?" I inquired, trying to correct her without outright correcting her.

"Accepting, I guess," she said.

I said nothing more, because if I had opened my mouth I wasn't sure what would have flown out. I'm not, by nature, an insecure person, but in that moment my mother-in-law, bless her speak-before-you-think heart, hit on one of my biggest insecurities: that C.J.'s being gender nonconforming, effeminate, and possibly gay is my fault because, as evidenced in my brother, I carry the "effeminate boy who will grow into a stereotypical gay man" gene. My mother-in-law said what I assume a lot of people think: that I should be thankful that my husband is a big enough man to not hold C.J.'s gender nonconformity against me.

"Well, that just means that you did something right," I said to her after some silence.

Later, I talked to my mother about the conversation on the phone.

"Well, if someone's to blame, then it's me, because I had Michael," my mother said.

We laughed. If the LGBTQ blame has to be placed on someone, then we are your girls. I had been doing some research on my mother's side of the family and had recently realized that if I raise a straight son, I will allegedly be the first woman in three generations to do so. From the looks of the gay branches on our family tree, we raise gay boys. I can see why the LGBTQ blame—if it must be placed—would be placed on us.

Also during that trip, we decided to tell Matt's parents about the blog, which was six months old. I probably should have told them about it earlier and not kept that part of our lives from them, but I was still in hiding about the blog and, sometimes, about C.J. Every once in a while, when we caught up with each other on the phone, my mother-in-law would ask, "Is C.J. still playing with dolls?"

It was a simple question. It wasn't said with a connotation

one way or another. My mother-in-law was curious, not con-
niving. She just wanted to know about her grandchildren, but
I took it personally. As though if I said yes she would question
my parenting and me, and if I said no I would be lying, and if
she seemed relieved I would be disappointed.

"I started a blog about raising C.J.," I said as my in-laws,
Matt, and I were sitting around the table one night doing a
thousand-piece puzzle.

"What's a blog?" they asked.

"It's like a journal online that other people can read."

"We're not on Facebook," my mother-in-law stated matter-
of-factly as she tried to force a puzzle piece to fit where it obviously didn't.

"It's not Facebook. It's like a website where I can write
whatever I want." This might be pointless.

"On the interweb?" Yep, probably pointless.

"Yes, the Internet," I clarified.

"Are we blocked from seeing it, like Facebook?" Interesting. Apparently they had attempted to get on Facebook at
some point.

"No, it's not blocked. You can see it," Matt said.

"We don't really go on the Internet, and we definitely don't
do Facebook."

The subject changed seamlessly to talk of the weather,
cinnamon bears being more aggressive than black bears, and
the neighbor up the street who loved his hunting dog more
than his wife. My father-in-law asked my mother-in-law if
she needed a mallet to pound the puzzle piece into the spot it
wasn't shaped for.

"You know, our good friends told us that you were writing inappropriate articles about C.J. in the newspaper. This must be what they were talking about," my mother-in-law said after a few more random mini conversations had run their course.

My heart sank into my stomach, which dropped to my knees, which started to shake. My face flushed as I felt anger and sadness. I set down the puzzle pieces that had been in my hand.

Every day people disagree with my choice to chronicle my adventures in raising C.J., and my skin has grown thick, but when the criticism comes from closer to home, the pain is fresh.

"Not everybody agrees with my decisions initially, but if they really take the time to read my writing, they usually change their mind. You know, I actually kind of have a lot of people reading my blog, and I feel like I'm doing something important," I explained. Matt was nodding his head in support.

"Well, I don't know. I don't go on Facebook. All I know is we're going to love C.J. no matter what," my mother-in-law said.

"Well, that's all that matters."

Silence absorbed the evening. One by one we left the puzzle table to retire for the night. The next day, my father-in-law snuck up behind me while I was on the computer they have upstairs.

"Can you add your blog to my 'favorites' tab?" he asked slyly.

"Sure," I said with a smile.

Nothing more was said about the blog or C.J. during that

trip. I later learned that after we left, Grandma and Grandpa Colorado read every single post. And after nearly a year of processing time and educating themselves, they became unexpected advocates. All of their friends know that their grandson is gender nonconforming. If those friends don't like it, they can take a hike down the unpaved road that leads from their home to the Continental Divide. Grandma and Grandpa Colorado are the first to call and tell me that there is an LGBTQ topic being covered on this or that television news show. In their volunteer work with disadvantaged youths, they've encountered and embraced a gender-nonconforming fourth-grade boy named Seth who wears headbands to school and loves Minnie Mouse. I get updates on Seth almost every week. Their evolution has been cool to watch as our multi-generational family has grown with C.J. and the special needs his gender nonconformity presents.

Chapter 20

THAT SUMMER, JUST BEFORE C.J. was to enter prekindergarten at Chase's school, I spent a lot of time reading and researching about sex, gender, sexuality, and kids. I was hungry
for anything having to do with gender-nonconforming kids,
how to best parent them, and what the future may hold for
them.

I got particularly absorbed in a book that had just been re-
leased titled *Gender Born, Gender Made* by Diane Ehrensaft,
PhD, which was written as a guidebook for raising healthy
gender-nonconforming children. I swear Ehrensaft is the pa-
tron saint of kids who don't conform to traditional gender
norms. She should be celebrated with a day off from work and
school; a Saint Diane medal worn by families with gender-
creative loved ones; a mural painted of her portrayed as a Pied
Piper type with a gaggle of kids of varying gender represen-
tations following happily behind her; or whatever it is good
people do to honor their beloved protectors.

Ehrensaft, a developmental and clinical psychologist who
has worked with gender-nonconforming children and their
families for the past quarter of a century, hoped to "carve

a path toward gender health for all the children and youth who go against the normative gender grain of our culture." She calls these children "gender creative" instead of the usual "gender variant" or "gender nonconforming."

Her book should be recommended reading for all parents-to-be; although it might scare first-timers, who probably haven't even considered that their precious little peanut could be a boy who wants to be a girl, or vice versa, or both, or something even more unique. It should be required reading for all parents and family members even remotely involved in the life of a child who plays creatively with gender.

Ehrensaft can relate to parents of gender-creative kids because she is one. Her grown son was gender creative and now identifies as gay. Before her, I had only read and heard from people who were "experts" on gender-nonconforming children through a limited amount of study and/or observation. Never before had I heard from a credentialed expert who had also actually parented a gender-nonconforming child.

She explains that "gender creative is a developmental position in which the child transcends the culture's normative definitions of male/female to creatively interweave a sense of gender that comes neither totally from the inside (the body, the psyche), nor totally from the outside (culture, others' perceptions), but resides somewhere in between."

Ehrensaft acknowledges the harm done to gender-creative children should they fall into the wrong hands. The wrong hands may belong to people in her profession, only a small number of whom "are just beginning to embark on a long project of reexamining what it means to be a gender-healthy boy, girl or other in the twenty-first century."

Her model for raising gender-creative children "follows the child's lead and goes where the child takes us. It assumes that the child most likely comes to us with his or her gender creativity intact, rather than being shaped after birth by hapless parents who have some gender-skewed agenda or are incapable of setting appropriate limits with their children and providing proper gender guidance."

That is, of course, what I like most about Ehrensaft. She takes the blame off the parents and makes a strong case for convincing others to do the same. She acknowledges that, "in the face of confusion, disapproval and outright opposition, it is a challenging, confusing and brave journey that parents embark on when gender creative children appear on the family scene." It was nice to have the blame and guilt lifted a little; I was able to take a breath.

She calls gender-creative children "blessed with the ability to hold on to the concept—that we all had one time in our lives—that we were free to be anything we wanted—boy, girl, maybe both."

Nobody besides Ehrensaft had ever told me that my child was "blessed" because he is gender creative; more often than not, they tell me the complete opposite. Ehrensaft made me happier than she will ever know. Then she terrified me.

> To be gender nonconforming is to risk being killed, but on a daily basis it more likely means being harassed, confused and misunderstood in the community or maltreated by mental health professionals. . . . There is no doubt that these children are among the ranks of minority individuals in our society who must anticipate bigotry and antipathy from those

who either do not understand, are ill-informed, govern their thinking with myth rather than reality or . . . project hatred onto those who are different from themselves. At the same time, gender creative children diverge from almost all other minority children in that they have an additional mark against them: they may face aspersion from their very own family, loved ones who are supposed to be their protectors.

I was emotional and thinking about the way in which I wanted to mother my gender-nonconforming son, when it hit me: what if I wasn't around to mother him? I mentioned my concern to a friend of mine whom I'd met through my blog. Gabrielle's son was gender nonconforming as a child. At about C.J.'s age he told her that he had "girl blood" in his boy body. Now he's a charming gay teenager who still likes to wear her heels around the house occasionally because he enjoys the sound they make on the hardwood floor.

Gabrielle told me that it's her biggest fear in life that something will happen to her and she won't be present to advocate for and protect her son. She said it's a fear I should get used to, because it's not going to go away. Gabrielle is beautiful and no-nonsense.

Sheer panic set in, and I decided to write a letter to Matt explaining how I felt and how I wanted him to raise C.J. if I were to die. Then I posted it on my blog for my girlfriends to read too. I let them know that I'd hold them accountable from the afterlife if they didn't help Matt stay true to my wishes. They thought I was being neurotic, but they read the letter and agreed to my demands.

To My Hubby,

I've never told you how much I worry about losing my life and leaving you and the boys behind. No mother wants to outlive her children, but no mother wants to vanish from their lives in their youth. Length of life is an even greater concern because of C.J., our little boy with uncommon wants and non-traditional needs. Sometimes, when he does something that only a mother could love, I get scared. If only a mother could love it, who will love it when I'm gone?

If something happens to me, and I'm no longer here to raise C.J., remember these things . . .

Enjoy the unique journey, even though I'm not here to hold your hand through it.

Seek out therapy for you, for him, for his brother. Create a solid team for raising our boys into men, like you and the ones that came before you. It takes a village to raise a child, but make sure to choose the village wisely, one that is well suited for C.J.

If something that he is doing is bothering you, think to yourself, "Why is this bothering me so much?" I've found that the answer usually has something to do with what other people will think or say. Remember, this isn't about you; it's about him.

Let him perform. Let him sing and dance and act until his heart is content. He may be the only boy doing it, but if it doesn't bother him, try not to let it bother you.

Let him be creative, which may mean trips to the craft

store. He wants to create and it's a messy process. Put down newspaper and let him go for it. It may require some direction and participation from you. Have fun! Sign him up for art classes.

Strongly encourage him to try sports. A sport. Any sport. He may not like the typical, considered-to-be-more-masculine sports, but there are other ones. Between fitness and the arts, he will have healthy outlets for release when he needs them most.

Get interested in what he's interested in. Fake interest. Just as you learned to properly identify all of the Disney Princesses, be able to understand what he is excitedly talking about.

Hold him accountable; there are no excuses.

Surround him with the right people. Protect him. Keep him safe. Be his advocate. You don't have to write a blog, but you do have to stand up for him. Stay engaged and stay in the know.

Support his spirit; never ask him to get rid of his love of make-believe. Make believe with him. Show him that anything is possible and believe it yourself.

Take him to museums and the theater and concerts and other places you wouldn't normally go. Continue to brush his hair as long as he wants you to. Keep his dress-up drawers stocked. It doesn't have to be fancy stuff. The Goodwill is good enough.

Raise him strong, with a sense of humor. Raise him smart, with compassion for others and their journeys. Things aren't "weird," they are just "different," and "different" isn't bad.

Raise him to know that if he needs to talk, you will listen. And if you don't understand exactly, you'll still listen and, then, try to find somebody else for him to talk to who might listen and understand even better. Find him mentors, no matter the subject.

Be his biggest fan. Your job is to love him, not change him. Support him. Let him know that you are there unconditionally.

Remember that holidays are for wonder and joy and impossible things. Create them accordingly. Get him the toys that he wants most, even if it means shopping from the pink aisles, not the blue.

Take pictures. Keep report cards. Keep his secrets. Know his friends.

Remember the names of all of his boyfriends or girlfriends or boyfriends and girlfriends. Remember the names of his bullies. Let the bullies know that you know their names. Never let others feel big by making him feel small. Volunteer in his class.

Encourage him to see the world and seek out inspiration. Buy him books. Hug him and kiss him and tell him that you love him no matter what every day, even if he doesn't want you to.

Teach him to respect his body and sex, no matter his orientation.

Help him be the best at whatever he wants to do: hair stylist, mechanic, lawyer, whatever. Whatever he wants to do, encourage him to do it well.

Let him watch *Dancing with the Stars*. If he continues to be a fan of Paula Deen, or, as he calls her, "The Lady Who

Cooks Dinner," take him to her restaurant. Eat the fried chicken and banana puddin' for me.

Tell him that I can hear him when he whispers to me and that I'm always watching over him.

Raise him to know that his mommy adored him and fought for him as he innocently played with his Barbies in the other room. Raise him to know that you will fight for him. Raise him to know that you wouldn't want him to be any other way. He's perfectly created as is. Never let anybody tell him any differently.

I'll miss watching you walk hand in hand down the street, you and the little boy in the black-and-white polka dot apron.

Love always,
Your Wife

Chapter 21

MATT AND I WENT THROUGH a really lonely time of transition as our family became more and more public and unapologetic about C.J.'s gender nonconformity. We weren't in hiding so much anymore. We had a name for his behavior, I had done my research and knew that we had to raise C.J. without attaching shame to the way he was created, and quite frankly, we were so used to C.J. playing with dolls and cross-dressing that sometimes we didn't notice it when other people did.

The friends we consider to be our chosen family stuck with us every step of our journey and continue to do so to this day. They want to be a part of our lives. We had friends choose not to be a part of our lives because of C.J. and our parenting style. And we had friends who we decided weren't healthy for our children or us. There were relationships that ran their course more quickly than usual. Homophobic people? Gone. People who judge negatively? Gone. People who seriously question our parenting? Gone. People who gossip? Gone.

We don't want to live a detached, disconnected, disengaged life. We welcome new families to befriend, but because of C.J. we've learned to approach new people with hesitation. We can't predict people's reactions to our wonderfully unique son. If people aren't cool with the LGBTQ community, they can't be a part of ours. If they don't want to have a talk about gender and empathy with their children, then they may not want to meet ours. If they could never imagine letting their little boy dress like a Disney Princess, then our son's special magic may be lost on them.

When C.J. started liking girl stuff and acting effeminate, life was good. We were just a little different, a little quirky. We were that family with the free-spirited redhead. There was no solitary ache.

Then we learned that a two-year-old boy playing with Barbies and dressing up like a girl gets far different looks and laughs from strangers than a five-year-old boy playing with Barbies and dressing up like a girl. Never underestimate the isolating and exhausting power of those looks and laughs.

Raising a gender-nonconforming child can be excruciatingly lonely, a tear-worthy existence that we walk through and try to shield our children from. Sometimes we feel like parents alone on a tightrope, surrounded by people who will watch and be entertained but who will not catch us if we fall.

There were two families we were friends with. Each family had two boys who were roughly the same age as our two boys. We used to get together and watch as the boys played with their light sabers, *Star Wars*–style. Two brothers against two brothers against two brothers. Except that C.J. didn't want to play. So it was two against two against one, Chase. It wasn't fair. Neither the game nor the fact that it made Chase feel like C.J. wasn't always on his team, didn't always have his back, wasn't always a true brother. I'd watch as Chase would get whacked from behind with two light sabers at once, and we'd go home.

Another family we were friends with had a little girl who was less than a year older than C.J., and her dress-up wardrobe was one of the best we've seen. C.J. adored her and wanted only to get all dolled up with her. Usually a dress-up queen, the little girl would watch C.J. awkwardly. She couldn't quite place him in a tidy category. Boy? Girl? Tomboy? Pink boy? Freak? She would hesitate and then wouldn't dress up when C.J. was there because she was uncomfortable. C.J. hoped, every time, that she would join him in make-believe. She wouldn't, so we went home.

Once, we arrived at some friends' house and walked into their side yard. We could hear them in the backyard playing baseball. Their oldest son ran over and told C.J. that he couldn't be there. He couldn't be in the backyard because they were playing baseball and C.J. didn't like baseball; he liked princesses. C.J.'s feelings were hurt, though he tried to hide it. It was uncomfortable. We stayed for Chase to have a chance at bat and then we went home.

Days later we were in the middle of a dinner party and C.J. ran to me crying and buried his head in my lap. He was wearing a flamenco-dancer skirt and was crushed that a male friend had told him that they couldn't be best friends anymore because C.J. liked girl stuff. Everyone has feelings; everyone is tender—C.J. more so than other boys his age. His feelings were so hurt and he was so embarrassed that he couldn't recover and we went home.

Friendships we had cultivated for years seemed healthy one day and wilting the next. Superficial friends have superficial questions. Is he still into dolls? Oh, that phase still, huh? Do you mind if he doesn't wear a skirt around my son? His hair is getting long; are you going to cut it? Why does he like girl colors? Why do you let him do that? When do you think he'll be more "boy"? What are you going to do with him?

Real friends ask real questions. How are you all doing? Does he get teased? Is it hard for you, for him, for Chase? What do you worry about most? Do you think he's transgender? How is his brother doing with it all? How does it affect your marriage? What can I do to help?

We want honest connections with people but have learned that sometimes our gender-nonconforming child and the way in which we have chosen to raise him get in the way. We've noticed a lot that the elephant in the room is our son.

The demise of my relationships with other women and mothers has been the most emotional. I grew up with a cousin who had Down syndrome. As I watched my aunt raise her, I became aware that parenting a child with special needs was equal parts rewarding and challenging. I learned that sometimes a mother has a tough day . . . or a hundred, all in a row. On those days, she needs her best, strongest, most loyal women friends to pop over for a glass of iced tea on the patio (or a smoke in secret on the side of the house, from what I saw while snooping).

From my perspective, nothing bonded women like motherhood. When a member of your female inner circle has a baby, that baby becomes a child of the group automatically with all the rights and privileges.

Decades later I watched my best friends struggle with motherhood in all sorts of ways: infertility, miscarriages, stillbirths, adoption, kids with special needs, and perfectly happy, healthy kids who left my friends—their mothers—feeling threadbare. In some instances, as lovely as a husband or partner may be, there is no substitute for the friends in a mother's life.

I had been blessed with amazing relationships with stellar women. It had been reinforced to me that women assemble in a time of need, especially when motherhood and children are involved. But I didn't fully understand the power of women and friendships until I was the gal who needed them most, because I was raising a boy who wanted to be a girl.

For the most part, the women in my life have gladly stepped up to my family's unique challenges, loving C.J. and answering my late-night phone calls and texts when sleep eludes me and worry about my son and his future takes hold of my heart. My friends have rallied around us. They are a group of women that I wouldn't trade for anything in the world.

Some of my friends have disappointed and hurt me greatly—women I considered to be my forever friends, women who were the "additional emergency contact" in my son's school file. With them, it was more than superficial stuff like sharing a bottle of wine, a closet, or a secret; it was about sharing a life. But when my son started wearing dresses, I guess for some my life wasn't worth sharing.

Other women and mothers have questioned my parenting skills plenty. What kind of mother lets her son wear red Mary Janes to ride his purple scooter in plain view? I do. What kind of mother French-braids her son's hair? Me. What kind of mother lets her son have a princess-themed birthday party and, when asked, suggests that guests gift him with anything they would buy for a girl his age? This mother, this one right here.

We make strangers feel uncomfortable. I get that. But when we started making some of my closest friends uncomfortable, I struggled to understand the unexpected negative judgment they cast my way. We were the closest of friends, mothers doing the best we could, helping one another at every turn. Then, suddenly, we weren't.

One girlfriend of mine had two boys who both loved C.J. when they first met, when C.J. was more boy than girl. As C.J. shifted, so did they. They got mean. I talked to my friend about their behavior and asked if she had ever talked to her sons about C.J.'s being different.

"No," she said.

"Maybe it's time," I said softly but seriously.

"I'm not going to do that. I'm not going to talk to my boys about gender and homosexuality," she replied sternly. She'd been thinking about it, I could tell.

"This isn't about gender or sexuality; this is about empathy," I said, in shock. Treat others how you want to be treated. It's that simple.

She shook her head "no" sadly. I walked out of her house, the one I had previously always entered without knocking, and cried big, fat, silent tears.

"Do you ever feel like you're raising a special-needs child?" a friend asked me.

"Yes, but I feel bad saying it," I admitted.

"You shouldn't," she assured me. "My husband and I say all that the time that we don't know how you do it, we don't know what we would do if we had a son like C.J."

Special-needs kids are often defined by what they cannot do. My son cannot blend in. He cannot wear boring socks. He cannot resist having his nails painted. He cannot stop dancing when music comes on. He cannot resist the urge to strike a pose for the camera. He cannot play pedestrian games like cops and robbers or cowboys and Indians. He cannot shun a good skirt with lots of "twirl" to it. He cannot choose to play with a group of boys over a group of girls. He cannot keep his hands off beautiful hair. He cannot say no to a great craft. He cannot turn away from things that sparkle, glow, shine, or have a good use of color. He cannot conform to traditional gender roles. No way, no how.

I love him for all of his "cannots," and I need our inner circle, our chosen family, to feel the same. As we were getting ready to enter prekindergarten, some of my friends let on that C.J.'s effeminate shenanigans no longer seemed innocent and were becoming disturbing. And so my inner circle got smaller but stronger. The women who were left are powerful, sassy, loving, sincere, protective, trustworthy, and all-around fierce. They are iced-tea-on-the-patio (secret-smoke-on-the-side-of-the-house) kind of women.

Chapter 22

"I JUST WONDER WHAT all the other moms at school are going to think when they find out about C.J. and your blog," a mom from school said to me as the sun was setting on summer.

"Well, if they do find out, I'll know who told them," I said and walked away.

Some people did know or were finding out about the blog, which I was okay with as long as they didn't talk to me about it. At that point I was guarded and didn't want to talk to other moms about it unless they could somehow relate. Otherwise it felt like I was giving fuel to the gossipy text/e-mail/social media/phone tree that included all the nosy mothers within ten miles, all of whom have their degree in child development with a minor in judging people.

This was not the tone I wanted set as we began counting down the days until Chase started third grade and C.J. entered prekindergarten. To say I was "a little apprehensive" about C.J. starting school would be an understatement, like saying Ryan Gosling is "okay-looking" or the Hermès Birkin bag is "a tad pricey."

The day the kids go back to school—after a long, hot sum-

mer at home bugging me for entertainment and Slurpees—
should be a joyous one. It should involve walking them to
their classroom (trying hard to control my glee and the urge
to do a tap dance), speeding home, tackling the couch, and
watching reality television in my pajamas. It should include a
large plate of nachos for lunch and a nap. I have no shame. But
throwing a gender-nonconforming son into the den of four-
to six-year-old, gender-conforming lions had turned me into
a coward.

Would the teacher notice that there was something different about C.J.? How could she not? Would she care? Would
the other kids notice? Would they care? Would C.J. get teased?
What would I do, could I do, if he did? I wondered if I should
tell C.J.'s new teacher in advance that he is gender nonconforming. I'm always left wondering what the proper etiquette
is for raising a gender-nonconforming child.

Part of me felt like I should inform C.J.'s teacher prior to
the first day of school, but I always feel a little uncomfortable labeling him to someone before they've had the chance
to meet him. I could let her figure it out on her own, but then
I worried that during her learning process she might not be
tuned in to the teasing and bullying C.J. could attract. I know
that kids will be kids and part of growing up is being teased.
But C.J.'s gender nonconformity opens him up to even more
harassment, and I felt that his teacher needed to know sooner
rather than later to be a little extra sensitive toward my little boy.

Questions swirled in my head. Would telling her that he is
gender nonconforming help C.J. or hurt him? What was best
for C.J.? What would make the first days of school better for

him, so that he would continue to be excited about learning and feel safe in his new environment? What would make the first days of school better for me, so that I could nap and run errands peacefully without children or worry?

After getting the opinion of one of my friends who is a kindergarten teacher, I decided that talking to C.J.'s new teacher early on would be in C.J.'s best interest. C.J. learns differently. If his teacher were to do a lesson and separate the boys into one group and the girls into another group, C.J. might shut down if he were placed in the boys' group. Then again, he might not. He confuses pronouns a lot, because he approaches gender differently than other kids do, and getting pronouns right is a big part of the early school years. If he's asked to draw a self-portrait, he might draw himself as a girl. He might draw himself with a boy torso, girl legs, boy feet, and girl hair. What kind of grade would an art assignment like that get?

If a teacher were doing evaluations to rate his progress, maturity, and aptitude, messed-up pronouns, half-girl-half-boy self-portraits, and tuning out in a group of same-sex peers might indicate that he wasn't ready for the next step in education. He was; he just climbs the educational ladder a little differently, and the teacher should know that.

C.J.'s first day of pre-K at his new school was going to be a Monday. The Thursday before, I took an early lunch break at work and popped into his classroom to see if, by chance, his teacher was there preparing for her students. I opened the classroom door, and there she was. I hadn't really been expecting her to be there. It was ninety degrees out, but I froze. I had the door open. She was looking at me.

"Hi, are you Mrs. Meyer?" I asked. I was sweating.

"Yes," she said, looking at me and wondering who I was and what I wanted. I entered the classroom of miniature tables and chairs. I felt huge and awkward.

"Hi. I'm C.J.'s mom and C.J. will be in your class this year and I just wanted to let you know that he is gender nonconforming."

I'm an idiot. I'm a complete, fumbling moron, and now Mrs. Meyer knew it.

She was still staring at me with questioning eyes. She was probably thinking that I had Tourette's syndrome or some form of awkward social anxiety. Between my gender-nonconforming son and me, she most likely was instantly formulating a strategy to transfer us out of her class. I knew who wouldn't be a candidate for room mom.

I planned to sound much more pulled together, maybe even intelligent, and at the very least coherent. For days I had rehearsed the moment a thousand times in my head as I waited for sleep to find me at night (nights when I worried that Mrs. Meyer would be superconservative, overly religious, and/or totally homophobic). In the moment, as I revealed a huge family secret to a stranger, my brain and mouth failed me. I felt like there could be no small talk because I was bothering her during her private time.

"Okay," she said.

"So, I just wanted to let you know that we are aware of it and we are okay with it and we are doing our best."

Now I was just trying to fill the silence and wasn't at all following the list of key message points I had developed. I had sweat through the armpits of my shirt. A wacky mom with pit stains. I had really expected more from myself.

"What exactly does 'gender nonconforming' mean?" she asked.

I explained—that I could do. Thankfully, I could count on her to keep this premeditated conversation on track.

"What do you want from me? How can I help?" she asked with a sympathetic look that locked eyes with mine and wouldn't let go.

I was fighting back tears and hugs, as I do whenever someone offers to be on our team and help us with C.J.

"Just help him to learn, get him ready for kindergarten, protect him from bullies, and have an open heart and open mind." There, finally something came out as I had practiced.

"I can do that," she said. "In my twelve years of teaching, I can't say that I've ever had a 'gender-nonconforming' student. So there is some research for me to do. And I may have some questions," she said thoughtfully.

"I welcome questions. Please don't hesitate to ask. I really do enjoy answering them," I said honestly. "And, of course, we really hope that you'll protect the privacy of our family to the extent that you are able."

We talked a while longer. We discussed how C.J. might learn differently and doesn't do well when groups are divided by sex. I think she stopped thinking I was a lunatic and started realizing that I have an uncommon and, at times, tough parenting situation. As we wrapped up our conversation, she thanked me for telling her about C.J. I walked out smiling, discreetly holding my arms out to my sides, trying to get my armpits to dry before I got back to work.

Chapter 23

IT WAS THE FIRST TIME my two boys would be attending the same school. Understandably, Chase was a little nervous about what C.J. would do to his social status. He was in third grade, after all, king of the lower-graders and big man on the small playground. If you walk onto campus with a brother wearing Tinker Bell boots and carrying a Disney Princess backpack, suddenly you aren't as cool as you once thought. We had to modify C.J.'s wardrobe a little for school that year.

If C.J. had been going to his own school with only three- and four-year-olds, he might have been a little freer to be, well, C.J. But this school year he walked onto a campus with more than a thousand kids aged four and a half all the way to worldly twelve-year-olds who shave, stalk people on Facebook, and make out near the drop-off zone using an excessive amount of tongue.

Three- and four-year-olds aren't exactly wise enough to know that C.J. is different. Tweens are, and they'll point out C.J.'s difference to him, to his brother, and to one another. So C.J. couldn't have the Disney Princess backpack he wanted and he couldn't wear his Tinker Bell boots to school. His backpack from last year was in fine shape, and he'd use it until he really needed a new one. He couldn't wear Tinker Bell boots to school because they weren't safe for the playground. Excuses and practicalities like those were often put into play when we didn't want to come right out and say, "We aren't comfortable with your wearing girl stuff to school. We are deathly afraid that you and your brother are going to be made fun of, to an extent that not only dulls your sparkle but ruins your life forever."

The use of excuses and practicalities was in full effect when we were back-to-school shopping. Now, having worn underwear for more than three decades, I fancy myself an expert on the subject. Yes, I know a thing or two about wearing underwear. And one thing is for sure: get caught wearing underwear intended for the opposite sex, and you're going to get a few double takes, and then some.

C.J. wanted Disney Princess bikini briefs, the pack with a different princess for each day of the week.

I consulted a few of my friends. I talked to my brother. The consensus was, don't get C.J. the princess underwear. That's also what my gut told me when we were talking late one night, especially because C.J. wanted to have the fabulous underwear to wear to his new school, with his new teacher and new kids.

What does it matter if he wears Disney Princess underwear? Nobody may see them. But what if they did?

In our family, we don't typically say that things are "for boys" or "for girls." At our house, Barbies aren't just for girls and Hot Wheels aren't just for boys. But I did it; I chose my words carefully and told C.J. that "they don't make Disney Princess underwear for boys."

"How come not?" he asked.

"You can't wear girls' underwear because there isn't room for your wiener and balls and it might hurt them."

We stared at each other, neither of us sure about the situation. I was hoping that that would be the end of it, as I envisioned the line of questioning that could come next. C.J. was hoping that I was wrong and envisioning his privates being crushed by princesses.

A few days after the underwear conversation, we were shopping at Kohl's for some back-to-school basics. Kohl's is a lot like Ikea, a sensory overload of products, unimpressive air-conditioning, no windows, and no doors. It's a retail panic attack. To top it off, there are never enough cashiers, the long line always gets dangerously close to the fine-jewelry counters, and my kids, if they manage to stay with me in line, like to wipe their dirty hands on the glass jewelry display cases and, on occasion, lick the glass to feel the warmth of the lights inside. When we walk away, it often looks like somebody smeared mashed potatoes on the glass.

On this occasion, the line was long, as always. There was a small elderly woman in front of me and an empty nester behind me. C.J. wandered a few feet away. He was up near the register where they display products that kids will want and parents won't.

C.J. held up a pair of pink fuzzy slippers.

"Mommy, can you put these on the list for my birthday?" he asked.

"Sure," I said, acknowledging the list we work on year-round. We put something on our imaginary list when I don't want to buy it but also don't want to argue about it. So it goes on "the list" for purchasing at the next gift-giving occasion. Our "list" could very well stretch from the West Coast to the East Coast and back again by now.

"Mommy, can you put this on my list for my birthday?" he asked, holding up a purple water bottle.

"Yup."

The elderly lady in front of me turned around and smiled.

"His birthday must not be near," she said, smiling.

"It's a safe six months away," I smirked.

"That leaves lots of time for him to change his mind or forget," she said.

I'd turned to see where Chase had wandered off to when I heard . . .

"Mommy, will these hurt my wiener and balls?!"

I turned to look. C.J. was standing about six feet away from me, in plain view of the entire line, and holding up a package of *Little Mermaid* underwear.

Chase returned to my side quickly, mortified.

I waved C.J. over because I couldn't think of anything else to do. I waved him over more quickly. He interpreted my wave to mean *I can't hear you. Say it louder.*

"I SAID, WILL THESE HURT MY WIENER AND BALLS?!" He enunciated perfectly and yelled loudly.

I was sweating and blushing and reminding myself that the whole scene would be funny eventually.

Everyone in front of me in line turned around and stared at me. I didn't even turn to see what the people behind me in line were doing. I'm sure it's safe to assume that they were staring as well. C.J. was still standing by the cash register holding the package of *Little Mermaid* panties high above his head and waving them impatiently.

I shook my head "yes" ever so slightly and smiled. Suddenly, I felt like I knew nothing about wearing underwear or raising children or standing in line. Maybe having them back in school, under someone else's care, wouldn't be so bad after all.

Chapter 24

FOUR DAYS LATER IT WAS time for Mrs. Meyer to meet C.J. He insisted on picking out his outfit: a polo shirt with wide pink stripes, purple-and-pink girl socks from the dollar spot at Target, and purple sneakers. Mrs. Meyer gave Matt and me a knowing nod, bent down, and introduced herself to C.J. He was wringing his fingers in nervousness. He waved good-bye to us and walked into the classroom.

The first few days of school C.J. came home and was happy but not completely thrilled with his pre-K experience. He said he played with the boys and it was just "okay." He said that when he tried to play with the girls they ran away and yelled "Ewwww, a boy!" Finally a little girl named Daisy came around and decided not to run from C.J. but play with him instead. That's when the girls realized what a fabulous friend C.J. could be.

C.J. soon settled into a routine at school and found his girlfriends to hang out with during free time. The crafts were fun, snack time was rocking, and life was good in Mrs. Meyer's pre-K class.

During those few hours when the boys were both in school

and I didn't have to work, I ditched the PTA meetings to do some online research about LGBTQ kids and school. My research online often takes me to scary places (where I've watched the world's biggest zit being popped, seen maggots living in a woman's nipple, and erroneously entered my symptoms into WebMD.com only to falsely diagnose myself as dying). Researching bullying and LGBTQ youth may have permanently scarred me. I found the Gay, Lesbian and Straight Education Network's 2011 National School Climate Survey, which found that more than 80 percent of LGBTQ students have reported being verbally harassed, nearly 40 percent reported being physically harassed, and nearly 20 percent reported being physically assaulted at school in the past year.

I hastily devised a plan in my head that would never come to fruition. I'd homeschool them. I'd brush up on my long division and get some workbooks from the local teachers' supply store and set up class in our family room. I'd always wondered why anybody would homeschool their children. Not anymore. I started thinking about field trips we could go on. The zoo. The park. The library. The salon for mani-pedis. With me as teacher, principal, coach, and guidance counselor, they might not be prepared for college, they might not be socialized, they might not understand a lick of math, but by God, they wouldn't be bullied. I could promise that.

My research continued. I read that the population of kids like C.J. has the highest rate of suicide attempts in the world. They are three to six times more likely to suffer from major depression, substance abuse, and unprotected sex. My at-home health-ed curriculum would have to deal with those topics extensively; we'd have to ditch history for that.

Then I read that "LGBTQ youth who believe they have just one school staff member with whom they can talk about problems are only one third as likely as those without that support to report being threatened or injured by a weapon at school or report making multiple suicide attempts." If I decided not to homeschool the boys, I would need to find them an LGBTQ adult on campus to confide in.

The next day I saw the vice principal patrolling the playground at recess. He was looking spiffy with his perfectly coiffed hair, pressed chinos, a denim shirt, and a Members Only–style jacket. I couldn't see his shoes. I started salivating. My dreams might be coming true. I was standing next to a mom who knows everybody's business.

"Is that the vice principal?" I asked casually.

"Yes," she replied all-knowingly.

"Is he gay?" I asked, ignoring the disgusted look that spread across her face.

"No, he's married with two small children. I think his wife is a teacher. I think she teaches fourth grade," she informed me.

"Shit!"

"What?" she asked, looking at me strangely.

"Nothing."

My only other gay-mentor-at-school option was the male fourth-grade teacher, the only other male on campus. I'd have to investigate further and keep my kids enrolled in school for the time being.

Other things I'd have to look into—which have proven to lower victimization rates and suicidality among LGBTQ youth—are peer support groups, nonacademic counseling, antibullying policies, a student judicial system, staff training on sexual harassment, and peer-tutoring systems. Can you blame me for ditching PTA? I clearly don't have time for bake sales.

One thing in C.J.'s favor? A supportive home. The increased risk for suicide is not because the children identify as LGBTQ but because of the way they are treated in their homes, schools, communities, and religious institutions. I had to make sure C.J. was treated well in those places.

I also started further researching the fraternal birth order effect, which my brother had alluded to some time ago in vague generalities (because sometimes he can't be bothered with details, unlike his sister). One of my blog readers had recently sent me an e-mail that simply said, "Fraternal Birth Order Effect. Look it up."

The fraternal birth order effect. It sounded superserious. Like a group out of *The Da Vinci Code,* a fraternity at Harvard, or a secret club of the überrich and hoity-toity. There had to be secret handshakes involved, aged scotch in snifters, dark wood paneling, and signet rings. Men in ascots for sure.

One night, when Matt was at work, in the quietness of the house after the boys' bedtime, I heard Google calling to me. I stayed awake until midnight (that's 3:00 a.m. in Mommy Standard Time) reading everything I could find about this mysterious term.

I found an article in the *San Francisco Chronicle* that explained the fraternal birth order effect in terms I could understand: "The theory suggests that during childbirth mothers may develop antibodies to proteins made by their firstborn son's Y chromosome and subsequent pregnancies may stir up those antibodies in an immune reaction that affects the development of a male fetus."

According to several studies I found, for each older brother a physical male has, his chances of being homosexual increase by approximately 33 percent, and birth order is the strongest known predictor of sexual orientation if you are a male (the same is not true for females). It holds true for boys born from the same mother but not raised together, but does not hold true for boys adopted into the same family.

After my Google fit, I couldn't stop thinking about all of the boys I knew who had multiple older brothers. I was counting little gay brothers to go to sleep. I thought of those shirts they sell that say, "I'm the Big Brother" and "I'm the Little Brother." The last-born son should have a shirt that reads, "I Have the Highest Chance of Being the Gay Brother."

I couldn't stop thinking about families with lots of boys. The Beckhams. The Jonas Brothers. The Kennedys. The Marx Brothers. The Duggars. Oh no, not one of the ten Duggar boys! *Lord, help that Duggar boy with a J name, and help him find our family if Jim Bob and Michelle tell him he's a sinner who is going to hell,* I prayed as I fell asleep that night.

In the next decade or so, C.J. may need a shirt that reads, "I Was the Last Son in My Mom's Uterus and All I Got Was This Stupid Sexuality." Chase may very well have taken up all of the heterosexuality my womb had to offer.

Then I thought, *What if science learns to alter the antibodies in the mother so that the likelihood of the fraternal birth order effect can be decreased?* Could women and doctors start messing with hormone injections during pregnancy to prevent homosexuality? Would women really do that? I knew that, if given the option, many women would.

I went back to the *San Francisco Chronicle* article about the effect.

"The fraternal birth order effect is limited to younger boys who are right-handed. In other words, if a younger boy has many older brothers but is left-handed, he does not have an elevated chance of being gay. . . . The right-handed exception to the fraternal birth order effect was particularly surprising because other research had previously uncovered another puzzler: Both men and women who are left-handed are slightly more likely to be gay," it said.

C.J. is the second son and right-handed. If he is gay, then the fraternal birth order effect holds true in our family. My brother is the firstborn son and left-handed; his handedness, not his birth order, was more of an indicator of his sexuality.

I was marveling at how I would have been more into science in school if we had studied the fraternal birth order effect instead of rocks, when I stumbled over to Wikipedia. There I read that the most likely outcome of childhood gender identity disorder is homosexuality or bisexuality and that stress during pregnancy makes the birth of a gay son likelier.

C.J. is the second of two sons born to the same mother. His being gay is 33 percent more likely than his brother's. Check. He has childhood gender identity disorder, which ups his odds of being gay. Check. My pregnancy with him included pre-term labor, gestational diabetes, and preeclampsia and was considered high-risk, which ups the child's chances of being

gay. Check. I'd had my suspicions about my son's current behaviors as predictors of his future sexuality, and now I had
scientific probability to back them up. Now what? Nothing.

I had been looking for some proof and hard evidence to
support my feelings that my son was a member of the LGBTQ
community so I could know what our family was dealing
with. Once I found what I was looking for, I realized that it
didn't change a thing. I still had no absolute answers, and I was
going to continue to raise my son just the same. I'd thought
that if I had the most-likely-to-occur answer to the question,
the question would go away. But it didn't, and suddenly it
started to not matter.

Chapter 25

AS SCHOOL STARTED, SO DID soccer season. We signed C.J. up for soccer for a few reasons. It's like a rite of passage. You never know where children will find their passion, regardless of gender, sex, or sexuality. Even as we began to indulge C.J.'s every gender-nonconforming whim, we encouraged him to give gender-conforming things a try, just as we urged Chase to be well rounded and consider dance, art, sewing, and scrapbooking as extracurricular activities. And yes, in the backs of our minds, never to be spoken out loud, Matt and I always had the thought that maybe, just maybe, the next "traditionally boy thing" C.J. tried might be the thing to reset his gender switch, get him more interested in "boy things," and provide the occasion when he really connected with boys. We weren't holding out hope by any means, but there was always a chance.

"Ohhhh, Mama, I look like a soccer player!" C.J. said. He was standing in front of my mirrored closet twisting back and forth at the waist, watching his shimmery black athletic shorts—which were two sizes too big—sway below the knees like a skirt as he moved.

"That's because you are a soccer player," I said with excitement.

"I am?!"

"Yep!"

"Why is my costume green? I don't like green. I like pink. And purple," C.J. said, not taking his eyes off his reflection.

"Because your team is called the Green Dragons!" I was trying to exude total excitement in hopes that it would be contagious.

We arrived at the first game, which is also the first practice when you're on an under-five (years old) AYSO team.

C.J. met his five teammates and his coach. They were all bouncing around like they were hopped up on Red Bull and Mountain Dew. A little boy named Nolan approached C.J., who was standing timidly by Chase.

"Give me five!" Nolan shouted aggressively.

C.J. smiled and gave him five. C.J. gives the passive version of a high five where you lay your palm out open and let the other person do the actual "fiving."

"Give me five!" Nolan shouted again. His energy was appreciated; it made me glad that my kids take a while to warm up.

Again, C.J. smiled and presented his palm.

"Now I'm going to give you a hard five!" Nolan shouted.

"No!" C.J. screamed and whisked his palm up to his heart.

"C.J. doesn't do 'hard fives,'" Chase said in warning to Nolan, who immediately turned and ran in search of someone to "hard-five."

The thirty-minute practice was over before C.J. knew it, and we headed to the game field. As we were walking, he saw it. I saw it. I saw him see it and I knew what was coming. He pointed to a little girl in a pink AYSO uniform and said very loudly, "Why does *she* get to wear pink and I don't?"

"Because you got picked for the green team. They don't have a pink team for boys. And this is one of those times when you get what you get and you don't throw a fit," I said. I've said that a lot, to both of my boys. I've had to say it to myself at times. C.J. was pissed, confused, and all-around disgruntled about the color of his uniform, but he kept walking to his field.

If you've seen kids this age play soccer, you know what it looks like. A cluster of children, with the ball in the middle, moving up and down the field and sometimes off the field, in a swarm of chaos and kicking that accomplishes next to nothing. They kick the ball in the direction of whichever goal is closest, with little regard to whether it is their goal or not.

C.J. followed the swarm of players and stayed on the outskirts, prancing and acting like he really wanted to kick the ball, but I could almost hear his thoughts whispering to the ball, *Please don't come to me. Please don't come to me.*

At halftime, which was a grueling fifteen minutes into the game, the kids were a sticky, sweaty mess with a coating of wet morning grass. C.J. joined his fans for a drink of water and some oranges. His shirt had come untucked in the frenzy of soccer action, and he was twisting it around in his fist.

"Mama, can you tie my shirt in a knot right here. I think it will be better that way," he said, indicating that he wanted his shirt in a knot on his right hipbone.

"Did you teach him that?" Matt gave me a questioning look.

"No, I didn't teach him to knot his shirts. Have you ever seen me knot my shirt? I haven't since the late 1980s, early

1990s, when I wore a banana clip in my hair," I said in my own defense.

"Then where did he learn it?" Matt asked.

"I don't know!" I said, turning to C.J.

"No, baby, we aren't going to tie your jersey in a knot in the front," I said.

"Can we knot it in the back?" C.J. asked, demonstrating how it would be done.

Matt looked at me and rolled his eyes.

"No, baby, let's just tuck it in again."

Halftime was over, so there was no debating which would look better, a retuck versus a knot in the front versus a knot in the back.

C.J. continued to follow the cluster of players, keeping to the perimeter, with his arms straight down and wrists at ninety-degree angles. At one point another player kicked the ball and it bounced off C.J.'s shin. He looked at us and smiled. Dimples deep and pride high.

"Good kick, C.J.!" we all cheered from the sidelines.

On the way home, C.J. recounted how that bounce off his shins was a kick that almost scored a goal, and I thought about how his sporty jersey had almost been turned into a one-of-a-kind knotted creation sure to go against AYSO boys' league standards.

The next year when it came time to sign up for soccer, C.J. politely declined.

"No, thank you. Too much running, and they don't have a pink team for boys."

After soccer season C.J. played baseball, which I thought might spark something in him. C.J. was born with baseball in his blood. His maternal great-grandfather was drafted by the Chicago White Sox in the 1930s. His maternal grandfather traveled Latin America playing in the Pan American Games. His paternal grandfather spent nearly thirty years coaching youths who went on to play in the pros. Matt turned down a possible baseball scholarship to play football in college. Even I was a decent shortstop in my days playing fast-pitch softball on a team named Sweet Poison.

Then again, Michael struck out at T-ball, and C.J. is more like Michael than anybody else in our family.

When we were kids, Nana Grab Bags would sit in the stands every weekend with her Farrah Fawcett hair and Gloria Vanderbilt jeans and cry behind her enormous sunglasses— this was the early eighties, mind you—as her baby boy struck out at T-ball while every other player easily managed to hit the stationary ball off the stationary tee adjusted perfectly within his strike zone.

Michael didn't seem to mind. He loved to pick daisies in the outfield and tap-dance for the bees. He was completely oblivious to the game being played. When the innings dragged on, he kept himself busy by reenacting both fantastic acts of *Annie* and singing all of the songs from memory. Flourishes were added here and there for dramatic effect.

Every once in a while he would grab himself and hop around yelling—so loudly that spectators at neighboring fields could hear him—"Mom-meeeeee, I have to go peeeee-peeeee."

C.J. had been watching Chase play T-ball and baseball for most of his life. He loved to be at the baseball fields, playing with the other siblings and getting Icees from the snack bar.

"When am I gonna play baseball?" he asked one day when

we were down at the fields. Soccer had just ended, so I signed him up immediately and he started playing a few short weeks later.

At the field they assembled the kids. C.J.'s hat fell off. He put it back on and looked at me.

"Does my hat still look okay, Mama?" he shouted across the field.

"Yes, baby."

"Do I still look like Strawberry Shortcake?"

"Yes, baby."

The other moms looked at me.

"Spread your legs, get down, and get 'baseball ready,'" his coach instructed.

Apparently C.J.'s legs don't spread. His knees were stuck together. With them tightly connected, he bent over with his little rump sticking out. His conjoined knees went from one side to the other to totally in the way as he tried to lower his hand-me-down glove to the ground. A grounder rolled passed him.

"Oh, my!" he exclaimed.

"Oh, dear!" he breathed as he ran after the ball.

C.J. playing T-ball looked as natural as Hannibal Lecter trying to give a heartfelt sermon at the local megachurch.

C.J. got our congratulations and praise for sticking with it, but at the end of the six-week season he decided that he didn't want to sign up for T-ball again either. That was fine; we'd let him consider it again at a later date.

Chapter 26

C.J. HAS, FROM THE TIME he was two and a half, had us in a state of constant learning, stretching, and growing. At age four he was among the youngest members of the LGBTQ community. That's a bold statement to make, not because someone might argue that there are younger members but because some people don't feel comfortable with my assigning my son to that group. Regardless, though it may not necessarily be forever, I feel like C.J. belongs to the LGBTQ community right now. The community, because of its obvious, heavy focus on sex, gender, and sexuality, has had the most resources and support for our family.

After my brother came out and I became a straight LGBTQ ally, I learned that transgender and transsexual people put the *T* in LGBTQ. But I always kind of ignored the *T* in LGBTQ. It didn't apply to my family or me. It's funny how you do that, ignore something you think has nothing to do with you, and then, suddenly, one day it pertains to you and you wish you hadn't turned a blind eye all those years. You wish you had paid a little more attention, educated yourself, because now you need to be informed.

That fall, our family had a particularly rough couple of weeks during which C.J. repeatedly said, mostly to Matt, that when he grew up he was going to be a girl.

"Does he say that to you?" Matt would ask me.

"No."

"Well, why does he say it to me?" Matt asked.

"I have no idea."

I wasn't much help to my husband, but I kind of felt like C.J. was testing Matt. Maybe C.J. felt that I really would—as I told him every day—love him no matter what. Maybe he didn't get that unconditional love vibe from Matt. Matt has it, but maybe C.J. needed to feel it more. I explained that to Matt, letting him know that all I could do was guess.

What do you say to your little boy when he says that when he grows up he will be a girl, in much the same way kids say that when they grow up they will be veterinarians, astronauts, teachers, and doctors?

We questioned our parenting. Had we become so loose and fluid with gender that C.J. was confused about the natural order of things? It's undeniable; most boys do not become girls when they grow up. Had we made it seem possible to C.J., as if he could just pick? Or were we confused and C.J. was trying to set us straight? Was our son one of those rare boys who are supposed to become girls when they grow up? How do you clarify with a child who isn't even five years old yet?

I was brushing C.J.'s auburn hair for school one morning during that time.

"Mama, are you putting my hair in long braids?" he asked.

"Ummm, noooo," I said, more than a little caught off

guard. His hair was "boy short" at the time, and I couldn't do much with it besides brush it and hope I could get his bed head to lie flat.

"Mom-meeeee, you're supposed to say 'yes.' I want long braids," he insisted.

"Ummmm, okaaaaaay," I said, questioning our interaction in my mind. Were we in real life or fake life?

Later that morning we were walking to school.

"Mama, am I wearing a jean skirt?" he asked, skipping along, holding my hand.

"No, you're wearing jean pants," I answered honestly.

"NO! I want to be wearing a jean skirt! Say I'm wearing a jean skirt!"

"Okay, okay, you're wearing a jean skirt," I answered quickly and obediently, not wanting him to get worked up right before the start of the school day. I was beginning to feel like I was trapped in some sort of weird alternate universe. I had no idea what game we were playing or the consequences it might have.

"Do you like my jean skirt?" he asked me coyly with a sweet smile, chin down, looking up at me through his lashes.

"Yes," I said.

I checked him into his classroom and got in my car, and tears started rolling down my cheeks. I wanted to call Matt, but I didn't want to upset him. In situations like these, I feel like I have to get a handle, get a grip on what's going on and break it to him slowly. I wanted to call my best friend, but I was embarrassed. What would she say anyway? What was there to say? Why couldn't my little boy just want to be a little boy? I wiped my tears away, took a deep breath, ditched the gym, got a full-fat caramel macchiato from Starbucks, and sat on the couch watching TV all morning.

That night we were putting the kids to bed. Chase was tucked in bed reading while Matt and I attempted to corral C.J. onto his top bunk. As he navigated the ladder, he looked Matt straight in the eyes.

"Daddy, guess what I'm gonna be when I get grown up?"

"What, buddy?"

"A girl," C.J. said, smiling. He locked eyes with Matt and held them there before ascending the ladder and plopping into bed between his Rapunzel and *Alice in Wonderland* plush dolls.

"Are you fricking kidding me?" Matt whispered to me as he pulled C.J.'s door shut. I shook my head "no" and told those early-morning tears not to trickle down my tired cheeks.

Matt left to work the graveyard shift and I curled into bed, willing tomorrow to be a new day—a day when my little boy didn't want to be a little girl.

A few days blurred by as C.J. wore imaginary girl clothes to school and I did his hair in imaginary braids every morning. He'd tell us, again and again, that he was going to be a girl when he grew up.

"I want to be a girl," he'd say dreamily, as if he were saying, "I want to be in love" or "I want to sit on a cloud and listen to the harp being played while eating cotton candy."

It went from unsettling to unnerving pretty quickly. Was he right? Was he trying to tell us something very serious and oh so real? Should we be proud of his imagination and our parenting that had taught him that anything was possible, that he was free to be exactly who he was created to be? Was he testing boundaries, expecting and needing us to push back? Matt and I both slowly, over the course of days, felt like we were going crazy. We lost sleep, we lost tears, we felt like we were losing our son, we felt like we were losing our minds.

I called my brother crying. Michael didn't know what to say. That's when I knew things were serious. He, like me, always has words. They may not be the right ones, but they are there and they are ready. But they weren't this time. I cried harder. I thought he might cry too, so I hung up the phone before I could hear that happen.

Why can't my son just be gender nonconforming and gay? If he's transgender, who's going to love him? Sobs and fear.

It's funny how your hopes for your child can shift so much depending on the circumstances. When I was carrying my second child, I wanted a girl because I already had a boy. Then I had a little boy who acted more like a little girl, and I initially wanted him to act more like a boy. I prayed that he wouldn't be gay because of the unnecessary hardships he'd have to face in life, hardships I'd watched my brother weather. Then I accepted him as a gender-nonconforming, girly boy and started to hope with all of my heart that he wasn't transgender. I started the bargaining process: he could be gay, just not transgender. All of this not for my sake but for his. It's not about me; it's about him. Mostly.

My brother called me back after he had had some time to think. We talked about C.J. being a little LGBTQer in the making.

"You know, babe, there are worse things to be," my brother said from his heart.

It was a wake-up call that put things into perspective for

me. It made me feel a little stupid. There are worse things to be than homosexual or transgender. I have loved the LGBTQ community from the day my brother announced that he was a part of it. But I wasn't acting like it.

Michael was right. There are worse things to be than LGBTQ. And although there are some parents who wouldn't want a child like mine, there are parents around the world who would trade parenting spots with me without hesitation.

Around that time, a family at my sons' elementary school lost their twelve-year-old daughter to brain cancer. Less than a year earlier, she had been diagnosed with two inoperable brain tumors. Their child was dying, they knew it, and they helplessly watched it happen. My child wasn't dying; he was just different. And while I might be mourning the death of my own expectations, I wasn't mourning the loss of his life. My child was here, healthy, and happy.

But still, when your son tells you that he's going to be a girl when he grows up, what do you tell him? What's the right answer? We felt that maybe C.J. just didn't know that boys grow up to be men and girls grow up to be women. Maybe he needed some education, some clarification. We could tell him that boys don't grow up to be girls, but because we know trans people, we didn't feel right saying that. If he is, indeed, transgender, we don't want him to feel like transitioning isn't an option. The hopelessness that comes with a trans person being told that they can never transition doesn't ever need to engulf our son.

Then we worried that if we told him that he could be a girl or grow up to be one, we would be allowing him to play too freely with gender, with no regard to, well, anything. We might be letting him choose to transition too early, to make a huge life decision on a whim and full of fancy, not because it was medically and physiologically needed but, as C.J. once stated, "just because it looks like girls have more fun." We constantly questioned whether the limitations we set as parents were either too constricting or too loose.

I felt like my mind and heart were going to explode. My family needed help. I kept thinking about a licensed clinical social worker who had contacted me a few times after reading certain blog posts of mine. She would often send e-mails in reply to what I had written or would leave a comment at the end of the post. She seemed genuine, smart, and spot-on with her advice. Her name was Darlene and her office was in San Diego, an hour and a half's drive from our home, which had always seemed too far. When C.J. started wanting to be a girl when he grew up, we decided that we'd drive to another state if we needed to help him; another county was a no-brainer.

I conducted extensive research (stalking) online to learn a thing or two about Darlene and to see if she was for real. Yup, she was for real. She has a bachelor's degree in psychology and a master's degree in social work. She is a member of the National Association of Social Workers and the World Professional Association for Transgender Health. She is very experienced in therapy with children, and when working with kids C.J.'s age she utilizes play and art therapy. She also assists parents in learning parenting techniques to meet their child's particular needs. Her website claimed that "her positive parenting techniques help to improve your relationship with your child, and help YOU to get more joy out of parenting." We needed to get more joy out of parenting, that was for sure.

Since 2006 she has been working with individuals who identify as transgender. Her primary purpose in working with such clients is to support the decisions they make about their identities and transitions, as well as to help them find confidence in themselves and their choices. She has a thorough understanding of gender identity issues and believes that most individuals seeking therapy for gender issues and possibly pursuing transition can benefit from exploring their inherent strengths and resources, as well as addressing any distressing symptoms that arise from the process. She has a lot of experience working with transgender youths, assisting both transgender or gender-nonconforming children and their families.

Do you know how hard it is to find a good child therapist? One whom you and your child both connect with? Now try finding one who has real experience with gender-nonconforming children and who is within driving distance. It's no easy task.

After conducting a background investigation worthy of the FBI, I called Darlene and we talked on the phone for a while. I explained to her what was going on. It was nice that she had been following our adventures on my blog, because I didn't have to give her a lot of background on C.J. or our family; she had read it all. She explained to me how she would approach our time together.

"Although I would be C.J.'s therapist, the bulk of my work would be with you and Matt to give you the tools necessary to be the kind of parents C.J. needs and so that you present a consistent, united front to him," she said.

That's exactly what we needed. We needed the help, not C.J. We took her first available weekend appointment. We loaded up the four of us plus Grandma and Grandpa Colorado, who were in town visiting, and drove three hours round-trip for a one-hour appointment.

Darlene is amazing. She's cute, hip, sweet, and spunky. If she weren't my son's therapist and there wasn't the whole doctor/patient thing going on, I think we could hang out and have fun. We would get our nails done while reading gossip magazines and then sneak off to a Starbucks and share a dessert. Or maybe we would meet up for dinner and each say, "Yeah, I could do a glass of wine," and that glass of wine would turn into two and a half glasses each and we would end up in Nordstrom trying on perfume and giggling uncontrollably at something that amused no one else in the entire store. Maybe we would go to a farmers' market.

But, alas, in the real world, I only see her once a month when C.J. has an appointment. The first half hour of our first session was adults only, Darlene, Matt, and me. I pretty much cried through the entire thirty minutes. Matt didn't say much for fear that he too would cry. We could hear Grandma and Grandpa Colorado playing outside with the kids.

I was afraid that my tears made me seem much more distraught than I really was. Yes, I was crying because I was hurting and scared, but I was also crying because I realized that, for the first time, we could really, truly bare our souls to somebody who understood our situation completely and could give us some answers and tactics to be the kind of parents our special child needed. I was overcome with the emotion of that realization. I was talking to somebody who could actually help us.

Darlene felt that C.J. wasn't getting consistent responses

from us. We needed to work on getting better at that. We determined that he was probably testing us at times and that consistency would be good for all of us. I couldn't help but think that it all stemmed from the times of intense bargaining and compromise that had consumed the first year or so of his gender nonconformity. He could have dolls, but only at home. He could bring dolls into the car, but not into the store. He could bring dolls into the store, but not to Chase's school. We had done so much slight shifting that C.J. didn't know where the boundaries were. We were keeping him guessing, when he was craving predictability.

Darlene asked us two questions repeatedly that helped with our worries. I began to hear her asking them in my sleep: "What are you afraid of?" and "And then what would happen?"

"What are you afraid of?"

"That he will get teased."

"And then what would happen?"

"We'd deal with it."

"What are you afraid of?"

"That he is transgender."

"And then what would happen?"

"We'd deal with it."

She helped us get comfortable with our son, our lives, and our future. And it was a huge bonus that C.J. took to her right away. Darlene's office is full of toys, and all of her doll toys are genderless. Babies with nothing on but white diapers, artists' mannequins with no hair or distinguishing features, and crazy superheroes that seem neither all male nor all female.

During the first appointment C.J. held up almost every doll and asked if it was a boy or a girl.

"What do you think?" Darlene asked back.

He'd tell her his conclusion. It was apparent from the start that he was hyperfocused on gender and trying to figure things out. I explained to her that he pretty much asked if everything was for boys or girls: toothpaste, toilet paper, soap, water. Darlene demonstrated to us how to answer C.J.'s questions with a question to take some of the pressure off us and put decisions back into his court.

"Mommy, are you putting a jean skirt on me?"

"I don't know, am I?"

"Yes."

"All righty, then."

We didn't have to give him the answers; he could give them to us. That made life easier. Eventually he didn't ask so many questions, because he knew that the answers were inside him.

Along with practical parenting tips, Darlene has always been happy to get into the nitty-gritty details of raising a transgender child. Kids who are initially gender nonconforming and later identify as transgender can go on hormone blockers to halt puberty to give them more time to decide what kind of puberty they want to go through. Once puberty is stalled and more time is bought, the vast majority of patients decide to continue with the transitioning process and take hormones to experience puberty as the sex that is opposite to their body but in line with their brain.

C.J. is a long way from puberty. He has a penis that he loves and identifies physically as a boy. We are a long way from knowing what the future holds or how this journey will end. Ten or twenty years from now, will I be the parent of two boys or one boy and one girl? I don't know.

In the meantime, Darlene is there to support and empower us to make the best decisions for C.J. and our family. There is no pain or distress in C.J.'s life, and we hope every day that it stays that way.

We were settling nicely into a relationship with Darlene when my brother introduced me to a friend of his named Callie who is a post-op transsexual woman.

I met Callie in a little coffee shop in the Silver Lake neighborhood of Los Angeles. I thought I would be nervous to meet her, but when the day came, I was eager and excited. I had a million questions for her. If I'd had to give our coffee date a title, it would have been "Everything You Wanted to Know About Transsexuals but Were Afraid to Ask."

I had no idea I was coming at the meet-up so aggressively, until I met the supercalm Callie. She's like a glass of wine, just enough to calm the nerves but not enough to take the moment away from you. She is more ladylike than I will ever be. She dabbed the corners of her mouth after taking a bite of her cookie; she sat with her ankles crossed and looked at me through the glass of her cat-eye spectacles. There's something vintage about her, with her crocheted shawl, beaded drop earrings, white-blonde hair, and perfect red lips. She's compassionate, caring, dainty, prim, and proper.

Callie was declared a boy at birth and raised accordingly. The problem was, her soul was all girl. She grew up in Nashville, Tennessee, with a minister father and a church-pianist mother. When she was C.J.'s age she wanted to be the Flying

Nun. She would blow on dandelions and wish to be a girl. To Callie, being a girl wasn't about getting all dolled up; it was about how the outside world treated you. As far back as she can remember, she has wanted to be treated like a female.

Her high-school test scores ranked her in the top one percent of her graduating class, but higher education wasn't something her parents encouraged. When the military came calling, she answered and pursued an assignment in the most feminine area she could think of: nursing. After her service in the military, she returned to Tennessee and began transitioning into life as a female. She explained to me that she is a transsexual, and I asked her to tell me the difference between transgender and transsexual.

"To me, a transgendered woman is someone who feels that she is fundamentally female, despite having been labeled as male since birth and raised as such by her parents. A transsexual woman is a transgendered woman who takes every step possible to align her physical form with her soul, which includes medical, social, and legal actions in most cases," she explained. "Of course, almost everyone has their own variation on what these words mean, but for me this was accurate."

Aside from the feelings of her youth, I was most interested in the transitioning process. I wanted total honesty and Callie gave it to me. She talked about unsafe black-market transitioning. She talked about poor, minority trans girls who had no love and support from their families and, as a result, look for love and support in dangerous places. They are girls trying to heal themselves from a lifetime of self-hatred, secrets, and shame.

"When I was transitioning, there were no mentors in being a

girl for the male-to-female trans community. It was like being a pubescent thirteen-year-old girl trying to figure things out, but with sexuality fully intact and access to drugs and alcohol. It's dangerous," she said, painting a dark picture for me.

She stressed to me the importance of not letting C.J. go through puberty as a boy if he is transgender.

"I wish I could have transitioned sooner so that I wouldn't have my height and broad shoulders. My biggest roadblock is my physical size," she said. I looked at her and could see she was right. I'm five feet nine and have felt like a big girl since high school, but Callie's size makes me feel petite.

She talked about the expenses that go along with transitioning as I hurried to write them all down.

"Sexual reassignment surgery alone is at least fifteen thousand dollars, and insurance doesn't typically cover it. That doesn't even include hormone blockers, hormones, therapy, feminization surgeries, oh, and a new wardrobe."

I stopped writing and looked up at her. She was smiling at me. I smiled back at her. A new wardrobe would be expensive. I wrote it down.

"It's never easy, it's never perfect, and it's never over. But it does get easier, better, and less important," she said of the transitioning process.

"Let's say that C.J. is transgender. What can I be doing now to help him? What do you wish your parents had done for you?" I asked.

"I know all too well the struggles one faces even in those earliest years of life, and how much of a life-changing difference it would have made if my parents had been supportive," she said, pausing to think. "Raise a confident child who knows that he is loved and that he will get love in the home, so that he doesn't have to go in search of it somewhere else. Raise someone who won't settle for dangerous relationships."

We talked more about her parents and how they still haven't changed the pronouns they use when talking about her, even though physically and legally she is a she. Their relationship is strained. It saddened me.

"They don't make an effort to recognize who I am. They should make an effort more than anybody else in the world," she said.

Yes, they should. All parents should make that effort, no matter their child, no matter their struggle. No matter what.

I asked Callie if she was in a relationship. She was, and it was new. I was interested in her boyfriend because I often wonder who will love my son, especially if he becomes my daughter. Everything else I can help him with, we can deal with together, but I can't find love for him; I can't help him fall in love and make that person fall in love back. What if, because he is different, he never knows a love other than the great big one he gets from his family? Callie admits that a woman in her situation doesn't find love easily.

Later I learned of a relationship Callie had as she was transitioning. She was a showgirl and he was a soldier. It was love and it was forever. On July 4, 1999, as Callie was being crowned Tennessee's Entertainer of the Year, her boyfriend was being brutally beaten to death in his sleep by two fellow soldiers in the United States Army. They beat him for loving Callie. They beat him because of a relationship they thought was "gay"; their minds were too small to understand that it wasn't a homosexual relationship. Callie's boyfriend was attracted to and loved women, and Callie was a woman, almost entirely. They were a boy/girl couple. It's a glaring example of how people can be so uneducated when it comes to sex, gender, and sexuality. And those ignorant people can be confused and fearful and overcome with hate. It is people like that I fear most in life, because they can and will harm my son for being different.

I found a quote from Callie on her website about her childhood that especially touched me: "I was just like a quiet, sensitive person who wrote poetry and walked in the woods and played violin and stuff. I wasn't delicate, really, but I wasn't really boyish. I think I just wasn't anything. I was so busy concealing everything that I just came out as a blank."

Two nights later, I had a dream in which there was a faceless child wandering lost through a forest in military fatigues with a pink skirt over them. For a moment his face fluttered into focus and I could see that it was C.J. I screamed and awoke. I don't want my children to feel blank. They can be the G or the T in LGBTQ, any letter in any acronym, pretty much anything at all, just not blank.

Chapter 27

AS HALLOWEEN APPROACHED THAT YEAR, I grew scared, knowing that my four-year-old little boy was going to want to dress up as either Dorothy from *The Wizard of Oz,* Alice from Wonderland, Minnie Mouse, Smurfette, or Rapunzel. He'd been talking about it for months. Think about it: Halloween is the one day out of the entire year when it's okay to dress up as anything you want to be. Obviously it's C.J.'s favorite holiday. Striking a compromise like we had the year before, with the polyester skeleton and face paint, wasn't going to happen.

"Why don't we do a male interpretation of Dorothy from *The Wizard of Oz?*" asked my brother. "I could custom-make blue-and-white gingham lederhosen, and we could get red Converse high-tops, and I'll completely bedazzle them with red rhinestones."

"Oh, yeah, that sounds really tame, like it totally would draw less attention to us than my son just cross-dressing out in public," I said sarcastically into the phone before exchanging good-byes. My creative brother was just trying to help.

I remembered back to 1984 when Michael convinced a

seven-year-old me to dress up as Tina Turner for Halloween. This was post-Ike-Turner-divorce Tina Turner. This was *Private Dancer* Tina Turner. This was reinvented-woman-ready-to-reclaim-her-fame-and-sex-appeal Tina Turner. I was a second-grader and the whitest girl in our ghetto Los Angeles neighborhood.

For some reason my mother let my brother have total freedom when it came to assembling my costume. Probably because she loved Tina Turner just as much as he did. Every weekend my mother would drive us around town in her brown VW Vanagon and we would sing along to "Private Dancer" and "What's Love Got to Do with It?"

My Tina Turner Halloween costume consisted of a short denim skirt, a tight white wife-beater tank top, and a jean jacket. My brother couldn't find legit women's high heels in my tiny size, so I was forced to wear the hard, plastic kitten heels that were supposed to be for playing dress-up only. The shoes were neither comfortable nor safe for trick-or-treating outside, but nobody seemed to care. My brother blew up two orange water balloons with air and stuffed them in the front of my shirt. I have to admit, I liked having boobs. They were my favorite part of the outfit and much larger than the real ones that grew in years later. On top of my head was an adult-sized light brown spiked shag wig. As with most of the enormous wigs that my mother and brother put me in for Halloween, my face was completely lost and my big brown eyes peered out.

Early on Halloween evening, while the sun was still out, my brother and mother made me stand on the front lawn of our house and pose for the entire neighborhood to see while they took pictures and laughed. I was stiff at first.

"Be more Tina Turner!" my brother yelled at me, coaching me through the photo shoot.

"Sing 'What's Love Got to Do with It?' " he shouted as he and my mother started laughing.

"Stop laughing at me!" I insisted.

"We're not laughing at you, honey, we're laughing with you," my mother said, stifling a chuckle.

I didn't see how that could possibly be the case when I clearly wasn't laughing.

Halloween was so much easier before my kids had opinions, back when I got to pick their costumes. I'm sure it's also an easy holiday for people raising boys who want to wear "boys' costumes" for Halloween.

If C.J. were an only child, we might let him get all dolled up in full drag and rock the hell out of All Hallows' Eve. The church's harvest carnival? Snap! The community center's trick-or-treat night? Werk! The local mall's pumpkin party? Fierce!

But C.J. isn't an only child. While C.J. might not get teased if he wears a "girls' costume," Chase would. While other kids may not even know that it's a boy under all that pageantry, Chase would. My heart often breaks for both of my boys.

I caught Chase on a bad day when I tried explaining to him that Halloween is for dressing up any way you want and that everybody in our house is free to pick the costume of his or her choice.

"Then I pick not to dress up," Chase said matter-of-factly.

"Then you might not get any candy," I warned.

"That's fine. I'll stay here and pass out candy and eat it," he said with a twinge of bitterness, his eyes avoiding mine.

"Do you really not want to dress up? Because that's fine. Or do you not want to be with C.J. if he dresses in a girl costume?"

"It's C.J."

Just as I had suspected. In a lot of ways, having a gender-nonconforming little brother forces Chase to make choices he shouldn't even have to think about. He has to deal with issues that most third-graders don't have to. Especially on Halloween.

To make matters worse, I talked to C.J.'s teacher, Mrs. Meyer, about her plans for celebrating Halloween in class. She confirmed my worst suspicions. Students in pre-K wear their costumes to school. Great. Perfect. It was the first year that C.J. and his brother were at the same school, and it would be the first time that C.J. would have the opportunity to wear his Halloween costume to school. We discussed having two costumes, but C.J. hated that idea and refused.

Michael and I had another brainstorming session. C.J. could be Tim Burton's version of the Mad Hatter, with the long, wild hair, a big hat, makeup, and a fabulous velveteen jacket with an ascot, or Captain Jack Sparrow with long braids, heavy guyliner, jewelry, and a peasant top.

"Any other Johnny Depp characters you'd like to throw out there for consideration?" I asked.

"Edward Scissorhands."

"I'm not putting blades on his hands. Besides, how would he grab the candy?"

I gave C.J. the options of the Mad Hatter, Captain Jack Sparrow, a member of KISS, and Adam Lambert.

"No way," he said, wrinkling his nose.

"What about a male interpretation of Dorothy from *The Wizard of Oz*?"

"What's an in-temp-ra-ta-tion?"

"Never mind."

I took C.J. to the costume store to select his Halloween attire. We went alone, in the middle of a weekday, so that we could concentrate on the task at hand and not deal with pesky onlookers.

On that particular day he really wanted to be either a prima ballerina (but "no buns on my head, Mommy!") or a cheerleader. Matt and I agreed that whatever C.J. chose to be, he had to have a wig. That felt safer to us. We both felt like we could really hide (I mean "protect") our child under a wig. A wig felt like armor.

We wandered eight aisles of options: boys', girls', and gender neutral. C.J. was not interested in any of the "boy" costumes, except for the moment he spent inspecting the size-extra-small Jesus getup, because, after all, it does have a dress and long hair. C.J. informed me loudly that Jesus's sandals are ugly, and I told him that it's not nice to judge Jesus or his footwear and that the options were limited in those days.

Then he saw it and our decision-making process was over; there was no going back. It was a costume he had mentioned a few times. It was Frankie Stein from the Monster High line of toys by Mattel. She is fifteen and the daughter of Frankenstein. She's supersassy and likes—according to her online bio—shopping for "scary cute clothes that are absolutely to die for."

Two elementary-school-aged girls were also looking at the Monster High costumes, until they saw C.J. trying on the Frankie Stein ensemble. Once they saw C.J. twirling in a dress, they could focus on nothing else. I didn't know that the eyes of a child could grow so large.

I awoke the morning of October 31 to C.J. jumping up and down next to my bed.

"I get to wear my costume to school! I get to wear my costume to school! I get to be Frankie Stein!"

I had talked to Mrs. Meyer to give her a warning that my son was going to be wearing a "girls' costume" to school. She was very thankful, and a few school days before Halloween she started reading books to the class about how Halloween is for being whatever you want to be. She wove in her own messages about fantasy and role-playing and how anybody could be anything on Halloween and not get teased.

We had been talking with Chase about C.J.'s costume decision and the fact that he was going to wear it to their school on Halloween. Because he is a great person, Chase quickly got on board with the whole thing. He agreed that anybody should be able to be anything they wanted on Halloween. It also helped that he was more focused on the awesome old-school-gangster pin-striped suit, fedora, fake cigar, and replica machine gun that he had picked out for himself. Plus, he saw how genuinely happy C.J. was in the Frankie Stein costume and knew that it was the right decision. He really is the world's best big brother.

On the big morning we drove to school and dropped Chase off at the "drop-off," because he's too cool to walk with us regardless of our gender nonconformity. I parked the car and

C.J. sprang from his seat and handed me his wig. I put it on his little head.

"Let's do this," I said.

"Let's bounce," he said, mimicking his uncle Michael.

We started walking to his class. We're doing this, I thought. My son is wearing tights, a skirt, and makeup to school for the first time. Kids and parents arrived. Nobody seemed to notice C.J. I held my head high and so did C.J. A little blonde Superwoman arrived and pointed at C.J.

"C.J. is dressed as a girl!" she said to a group of kids. None of them were as amused as she seemed to be. Apparently she made the announcement a few more times during the school day.

"Did that hurt your feelings?" Matt asked C.J. after school.

"No, why would it?" C.J. said.

Matt didn't answer. Mrs. Meyer let us change C.J. into "school clothes" in her classroom after noon dismissal so that we wouldn't have to parade C.J.—dressed as a girl—past his brother and hundreds of his classmates as they ate lunch.

A few hours later we were on the road to my best friend's house by the beach for a family-friendly Halloween party and trick-or-treating. By twilight my son was wigless, looking like a boy from the neck up and a girl from the neck down, approaching door after door collecting candy (which he would soon forget about and I would stuff into my mouth when he wasn't looking, lacking the willpower to throw it away or sell it to the dentist down the street for one dollar per pound).

"I wonder if people are thinking, *Lord, that's a homely little girl!*" I said to Matt while C.J. was up at a front door adding to his sugary loot.

"I didn't think about that, but thank you for bringing it to my attention," Matt replied drily.

There was a certain sense of comfort in the fact that wig on or wig off, we were thirty miles from home and felt a little freer to be ourselves.

Chapter 28

ONE MORNING IN NOVEMBER, while I was helping C.J. pick out his clothes for school, he got all serious on me.

"Mommy, today when we get to school, can you tell Gigi that I don't wanna be the daddy all the time? Sometimes I want to be the mommy."

"What?" I asked, confused.

"When we play house at free time she always makes me be the daddy, and sometimes I wanna be the mommy."

I stared at C.J. as a stream of thoughts ran through my mind.

The *nerve* of some little girl telling my son that he can't be a mommy! . . . Well, at this point, she's right; in reality it isn't possible for him to be the mommy. . . . What does it matter to Gigi if C.J. wants to be the mommy? She really is a bossy little thing! . . . Maybe C.J. needs to learn that he does have to be the daddy because he is the boy and boys are daddies. . . . Maybe C.J. can be the primary caregiver "daddy" while the "papa" is working the nine-to-five at some hip ad agency or modern design firm. Or maybe the "papa" to C.J.'s "daddy" would be a lawyer or doctor.

I remembered a little boy from my youth named Aaron.

He had stick-straight, baby-fine blonde hair that fell into his eyes. He had glasses and was tall for his age. We were in early elementary school, and I could always count on my persuasive powers to lure him toward the corner of the classroom where the pretend "house" was. There was a small kitchen, a bassinet, and an olive green rotary phone with a long, spiraling cord.

That's where it happened. That's where I could convince him—when none of the other boys were paying attention—to be the daddy, the token male who would play house with us girls. Finally, we had a traditional, nuclear family. I was the mommy and Aaron was the daddy. Sometimes we posed as if we were getting our family portrait taken in the Sears photo studio. He sat on a stool and I was behind him with my two hands on one of his shoulders while he held our babies in his arms. I played the part of the Sears photographer, too. The picture is still in my mind.

One big happy family. Poor Aaron. Poor C.J. He had a group of four or five girls he hung out with consistently at school. At free time they liked to play house and C.J. was always relegated to the role of daddy. This, to most, would be the obvious and only choice for him, unless he wanted to be the baby, but he is way too strong of a personality for that.

We were walking up to C.J.'s classroom and he started crying, which he had never—in his illustrious, two-year academic career—done. They were quiet tears, but they were there.

"What's wrong?" I asked as I knelt down to his level.

"Will you talk to Gigi?"

"I'll talk to Mrs. Meyer and I'll help you, okay?" I said. "I'll always help you."

His peers filed into the classroom and we hung out on the sidelines. Mrs. Meyer could see that C.J. had been crying.

"We're having a rough morning. Do you have a minute?"

"Sure," she said.

I explained the situation to Mrs. Meyer. I explained that sometimes when the kids played house during free time, my son wanted to be a mommy, not a daddy, and the girls in the class wouldn't let him. I explained that I understood both sides.

"I don't know how to handle this. I've never done this before," I admitted to her.

"Me neither," she said to me, and we stood quietly.

"I'm going to e-mail his therapist and see what she says," I said. I'm always open to suggestions, and hers are usually the best.

"Yeah, do that and let me know what she suggests," Mrs. Meyer said. "For today, I'll keep an eye on the situation."

"Thank you."

C.J. looked at us with hope in his eyes. Today he might get to be a mommy.

I e-mailed Darlene and she immediately proved why we adore her. I don't know how she got so smart, but I'm glad she did.

She said that we should step back and look at the bigger picture. "C.J.'s friends won't let him _____, and it hurts him badly enough that he cries about it." She told me to encourage C.J. to use his words to express himself to his friends, tell them that they are hurting his feelings, and ask them to stop the action that is hurting his feelings.

Simple enough, right? We practiced at home.

"I don't wanna always be the daddy. I wanna be the mommy sometimes, too. It's not fair that I always have to be the daddy," C.J. told me he was going to say to his girl friends.

I picked C.J. up from school the next day.

"How'd it go?" I asked him.

"Gigi said no. I can't be the mommy. I always haveta be the daddy."

I listened and observed. He didn't seem that upset. The next step was for Mrs. Meyer to talk with the girls to discuss the importance of taking everyone's feelings and opinions into consideration. It's a lesson more in empathy than in gender.

We can all use a lesson on empathy every now and then. I thought about looking Aaron up on Facebook to apologize for not asking him if he wanted to be the mommy instead of the daddy when we played house. I couldn't remember his last name. Maybe it's for the best.

A few days later, C.J. emerged from his class wearing his most victorious smile.

"I was the mommy today!" he proclaimed with a hint of shyness.

"Very cool! I'm so happy for you!" I said.

"Yeah, now our family has two mommies and two sisters," he said.

"Well, that sounds like a fun family."

"It's the best kind," he said as he climbed into the car.

Things were good for a while, and then Gigi really started to irritate me. She decided that because C.J. was a boy, he was not welcome to play with her group of friends at all. Boys were gross, and that included C.J.

I'd see her walk up to school, her five-year-old self in Seven Jeans or Juicy Couture velour tracksuits. She had top-of-the-line Ugg boots and True Religion shirts. She was too good for H&M. I didn't know that mean girls came in size 5T.

To make matters worse, C.J. wanted her attention and acceptance more than anything. He had to have Harajuku shoes because Gigi loved Harajuku Girls and Gwen Stefani. He couldn't wear his Miss Piggy socks to school because Gigi made fun of them. I hadn't thought that this kind of nonsense would start so young.

I strategized. I schemed. I decided to keep my enemies closer. I could live my life without Gigi in it, but C.J. felt like he couldn't. If C.J. wanted to be friends with Gigi, I would try to help him make that happen. I e-mailed Gigi's mom and invited Gigi out on a playdate with C.J. the following Tuesday.

That morning C.J. was beside himself. He was going to get to lunch with the most popular girl in pre-K. I picked them up after school and they scrambled to my car, all giggles and squeals. I took them to McDonald's. That would butter Gigi up. They got their Happy Meals with Barbie toys and sat to eat. We small-talked for a bit.

"Gigi, isn't it fun playing with C.J.?" I asked. She nodded her head "yes" and smiled at him.

"He is so much fun. He has the coolest toys at home and a dress-up collection and arts and crafts," I said, trying to make my son seem cooler in her eyes.

"Do you ever not want to play with C.J. because he is a boy?"

"No," she said and looked down at her food.

"Yeah, that wouldn't be cool," I said, looking away.

C.J. smiled at me.

"Wanna go home and have some fun?" I asked.

"Yeah!" Gigi and C.J. cheered in unison.

I had stocked the house so there was no way Gigi wouldn't have fun. We did crafts galore. We sat and did them and laughed and smiled. I was laying it on thick. We played dress-up. I took pictures and Gigi had me text them to her mom. We were having so much fun!

"Gigi was so nice to me all day at school today because she knew we were going on a playdate," C.J. said happily after we dropped Gigi off at her house. "I think she will like me now and will let the other girls play with me."

"I hope so, baby. We sure did have a good time." I was hoping for the best. Our afternoon had to have positive results, right?

Nope. The next day Gigi was her regular stuck-up self and C.J. was bummed. A few weeks later C.J. and I invited Gigi to hang out with us after school again. New day, same results. My plan didn't work, and it pissed me off. Gigi was not treating my son better as a result of our playdating. Matt reminded me how ridiculous I was being. I couldn't help it.

Not long after the second playdate, one of the sweetest moms from C.J.'s class approached me and asked if Gigi was ever mean to C.J. "Yes!" I shouted, scaring the infant in her arms. This mom's daughter, Lauren, was in C.J.'s group of girl friends from the first weeks of school, before Gigi had turned them on him.

"Oh, good, I'm so glad that she's not just bratty to my daughter," she said in relief. "And I even had her over for a playdate and she was really snotty. She told Lauren that she didn't like her outfit."

"I tried the playdate thing too," I admitted sheepishly.

"Did it help?"

"No." I admitted defeat. My white flag was up for all to see, even five-year-olds.

Forget Gigi, Lauren's mom and I decided. We started play-dating almost every week at the park after school so that our kids could form a friendship; it worked. Soon C.J. and Lauren were best buds and Gigi, feeling left out, wanted to play with them—and of course they let her; they are good kids.

I tried to pass on to C.J. the lessons Gigi had reminded me of: not everybody is going to like you, some people are going to disappoint you, some people have been taught to discriminate, and some people are pretty on the outside and ugly on the inside. When all of that happened to C.J., he still had a heart big and open enough to accept those people when they came crawling back in their miniature designer jeans. As his mother, I felt proud about that.

Chapter 29

AT THANKSGIVING DINNER THAT YEAR, we went around the table, giving each family member a chance to say what she or he was thankful for.

"I'm thankful for my family," Matt said to us.

"I'm thankful that we have a home and food, because some kids don't have that stuff," Chase said.

"I'm most thankful for my family, too," I said, smiling at my boys.

"I was thankful for my wig," C.J. said, sitting at the table with his arms folded and his head down. He was pouting because I wouldn't let him wear his Frankie Stein wig from Halloween to the table anymore, ever since that one time he'd gotten a ridiculous amount of ranch dressing in it at dinner.

"What else are you thankful for?" Matt asked.

"I'm thankful for toilets so I don't have to poop on the floor," C.J. said. Chase laughed.

"I'm thankful for stop signs so our cars don't crash and we don't die," C.J. said. Chase laughed harder.

"I'm thankful for American fags," C.J. said. Matt's eyes fixed on me.

"He means flags," I interpreted quickly.

"Let's just eat," Matt said as he cut into his turkey.

Days later it was time to deck the halls for Christmas. Matt was up in the attic handing down boxes of decorations to Chase and me. As each box was passed down, C.J. asked what was in it and Chase would reply by reading the label on the box. Two boxes came down that read "Angel," and C.J. nearly peed his pink pajamas.

"I LOVE ANGELS!"

"Okay, C.J., but we have to get all of the Christmas decorations down before we can start opening the boxes," I repeated over his screams.

He was bouncing around yelling, "I love angels!" while Matt was yelling, "It's too hot to be Christmas!" from the hundred-degree attic. Of course we had a heat wave in Southern California the day Matt had to climb to the hottest spot in the house and retrieve ten boxes of holiday heaviness so that we could celebrate a winter holiday. It's not exactly his favorite chore of the year.

C.J. finally got his wish and opened the two boxes marked "Angel." He squealed out of habit and then a look of slight disappointment overcame him. I don't blame him. The angels he had gotten himself all worked up over weren't my favorites either, but once upon a time, when I loved shabby chic and thought Rachel Ashwell was the world's most gifted interior designer, I loved them.

"When do we paint them?" he asked, referring to the angels that had been painted white and then sanded dull.

"We don't paint them," I said.

"But they are just white," he stated, unable to comprehend why a blank canvas would be left blank.

"Yes, angels are just white."

"That's boring."

Matt swooped in to put the angels in the spot they have occupied every Christmas for the past eight years. He obviously wanted to get the decorating job done so he could watch the football game that was on television. It wasn't helping that Uncle Michael was sitting on the couch watching Bravo.

"NO!" C.J. yelled. "The angels don't both go there. One goes there and one goes here."

He was pointing dramatically and moving things around and standing back to give his merchandising a better look. He was like a mini Tim Gunn in the workroom.

"The angels have both always gone here," Matt said, pointing.

"Boys, let's not fight," I instructed, as I do a few times each day.

Finally, with the angels in their places (one where they have always gone and one where C.J. wanted them to go), we opened another box.

"A STAR!" C.J. yelled as he picked up the gold star that perches on top of our Christmas tree. He held it high above his head with his right arm and marched through the living room, kitchen, dining room, and family room.

"I'm the Statue of Liberty!" he announced.

"C.J., please get back here and give me the star. I don't want you to break it," I said. Maybe I should have decorated when the kids were at school, as I had in years past. C.J. proceeded to run around the house with the star, being Lady Liberty, as I chased him.

He finally handed over the star and, when I wasn't looking, took two of our beaded and embroidered Christmas stockings and put them on his feet. They went up to his crotch.

"I'm an ice-skater girl!" he said. Sure enough, the glass beads on the stockings allowed him to glide on the tiled kitchen floor. A regular old Johnny Weir.

The next day we took Chase and C.J. to the mall for some shopping and approached Santa in the center court. C.J. started to simultaneously pull away from me and hide behind me. He ran in a circle around me as I ran in a circle around him, each of us trying to grab the other, while Matt and Chase looked on with amusement.

"I don't want to see Santa! I want to see Mrs. Claus and the reindeer," C.J. pleaded.

"Okay, okay, we aren't going to see Santa today."

"I want to see Mrs. Claus and sit on *her* lap and tell *her* what I want," C.J. insisted.

Great. Where was I going to find a place where C.J. could sit on Mrs. Claus's lap?

"There's Mrs. Claus," I said, pointing to Santa's photographer, who just might have been too big for the customary elf costume and had therefore been relegated to the role of Mrs. Claus—which is the role I would have wanted anyway because, one would assume, it comes with a little more respect and right to authority. But really, what do I know about the inner workings of the mall-Claus-to-elf employment org chart?

"She doesn't look like Mrs. Claus. She's not old enough. Where are the reindeer?" C.J. asked in a panic.

"They must be parked out by Nordstrom Rack," I mumbled as we cut through JC Penney to get to our car.

On the last day of school before winter break, C.J. took part in his pre-K class's holiday recital. He was so excited because all of the kids—boys and girls—got to be angels and wear white gowns they had made themselves from white pillowcases. Crowns of gold garland sat atop their heads.

I talked to Mrs. Meyer after the performance and let her know how happy C.J. was because all of the kids dressed the same and got to wear dresses.

"That was a well-thought-out decision this year," she said with a wink.

I hoped Santa would be good to Mrs. Meyer that Christmas.

That weekend, our family of four was at Knott's Berry Farm. Bless their berry souls for letting police and firefighter families in free between Thanksgiving and January 31. My intention was to get the boys' picture taken with Santa at Knott's. When Chase was younger, I had considered myself a connoisseur of authentic-looking Santas, and so I knew that the Santa at Knott's was going to most closely resemble the real deal.

We walked into his workshop and C.J. quickly realized what was going on. He began to wring his hands out of nervousness. He knew that if he was going to tell Mr. Claus what he wanted for Christmas, now was the time. The countdown to the twenty-fifth was in full swing, as evidenced by the dwindling number of chocolates in his advent calendar.

Chase hopped right into Santa's sleigh to shoot the shit for a while. He outstretched his legs and crossed them at the ankles;

he had one arm up on the side of the sleigh and was chatting up Santa about Beyblades, video games, and Percy Jackson. He knew that this Santa wasn't the real one and that C.J. wasn't going to get up in the sleigh anytime soon, so he decided to make himself comfortable and enjoy the stimulating conversation.

I finally convinced C.J. to sit on the steps leading up to the sleigh. He wouldn't look at Santa. Santa leaned across the sleigh, across Chase, and tapped C.J.'s shoulder.

"What do you want for Christmas, little boy?" he said jollily.

"Mama, what do I want for Christmas?" C.J. looked at me helplessly.

"How about anything Disney Princess?" I offered. Funny, at that point I was more concerned with helping my son capitalize on his big moment than with what Santa would think about my boy wanting a girl toy. How things can change in a year.

"Yeah, *anything* Disney Princess," C.J. said with a big smile, looking at me, not Santa.

"All right," Santa said assuredly as he tried to give C.J. a high five and C.J. ignored him. Chase compensated for his brother, giving Santa a double high five. The flash snapped and we walked away, looking at a photo of Chase leaning into Santa, giving a too-cool grin, and the top of C.J.'s head as he sat on the steps outside the sleigh.

C.J. might not have been specific with Santa about the gifts he wanted for Christmas, but he sure was with me. In the form of a list that was two pages long. Single-spaced. In comparison, Chase's list took up a mere half a page. Chase got everything on his list, and C.J. got all of the things he wanted most: the new Barbie, some Monster High dolls, a purple Razor scooter, and a jean skirt.

It was so much easier to shop for C.J. that Christmas than it had been the year before. We knew that our little boy was gender nonconforming and that he liked girl stuff most of all. We had seen the disappointment in him years before when he got "boy presents" and weren't going to do that to him again. This Christmas would be much better than the ones prior. We had learned a lot about our son in twelve months. We ended the calendar year not at all as we had started it, and we couldn't have been happier.

Chapter 30

WE RANG IN THE NEW YEAR and celebrated my first year of blogging. When I'd started the blog, I had committed only to doing it for one year, at which point I would reassess and decide if I wanted to keep writing. Well, when it was time to reassess, the holidays had just ended and I was exhausted. I had written about all of the noteworthy, thought-provoking, and amusing events of the past fifty-two weeks. I had written my reactions to and reflections on LGBTQ issues in the news and had kept a running list online of things I'd never thought I'd say to my son—like "Honey, your skirt is on backwards" or "Baby, you have on too much lip gloss." It was tiring, but from the responses, comments, and e-mails I received, I also knew that it was doing some good. I was fifty-fifty on the decision. Much to my surprise, Matt was the one who felt passionately about it.

"You can't stop. You're doing good for a lot of people and you're doing good for us, too." It's nice to have a raving fan.

"Oh, stop yourself. You know you can't just quit now. Don't be silly," my best friend said as I contemplated the decision with her on the phone.

Everybody else I talked with thought I was crazy for even thinking about shutting down the blog. I've learned that if everybody else thinks you're acting crazy, you probably are. I decided to keep writing.

My first year of blogging had been an amazing year of learning. We'd learned a lot about our sons and ourselves. We'd learned that for the safety of our family, we might have to distance ourselves from certain types of people. We'd learned who our real allies were, the people who would, no matter what, support us and join us as we took our journey and raised our gender-nonconforming, possibly LGBTQ son. Most important, we'd learned that we weren't alone. Our calendar was packed with playdates with other gender-creative families. I had built relationships with moms who traveled this path and were a little further along the road than we were and were now raising amazing young adults—yes, the once-gender-nonconforming kids are all now LGBTQ teenagers. I'd reconnected with people from my past who had been struggling with their gender identification and sexuality before my very eyes, without my even knowing.

I'd gotten a fresh perspective on the kind of father my husband is and was amazed. Raising a child like C.J. can tear a marriage apart, but I'd never felt more secure and confident about my marriage and the man I'd picked to spend the rest of my life with. We'd seen our older son start to "get it" and head down the path of being a really cool person who has an open heart and open mind. He's a boy who knows compassion, understanding, tolerance, and, most of all, fun. He gets things that a lot of kids his age aren't even aware of yet. In some ways he's years ahead with his innocence still intact.

We'd entered the warm embrace of the LGBTQ community and the community of families who are raising or have raised a gender-creative child. That warm embrace felt good; it felt like home.

We'd learned the deadliness of gossip and how it can poison good things. We'd learned that the person who gossips with you will gossip about you. We'd learned that prejudice can breed prejudice; hate can breed hate; and fear can breed fear. We still work every day to stop that breeding process in our family and to teach our children to be tolerant, even when the favor isn't returned.

The hate mail stopped. I had prepared myself for it to only increase with time, but the opposite happened. I think people got the sense that I wasn't going away. They were right. I think people saw, in the comments at the end of each post, that I have a huge amount of support. They were right. And I think that if people read even one blog post, they saw that I love my child and I'm just trying to parent in the best, healthiest, most loving way possible. They were right again.

I spent my first year as a blogger sticking to my twice-weekly publishing schedule pretty well, considering that I have a job, two active kids, a husband, friends, hobbies, a life, and addictions to social media, reality television, and gossip magazines (in that order). At times it grew tiresome, but on the blog's one-year anniversary, I published my hundredth post and knew for sure that I had it in me to write for another year.

Chapter 31

I PREFER THAT BOTH of my boys do at least one sport each season. For Chase that's not a big commitment to fill, but for C.J. it seems to be a little more inconvenient, to say the least. I want sports in their lives for a number of reasons: fitness, health, teamwork, and so that they learn new things. For C.J. it is important to me because I watched as my brother felt "not tough enough" or "not boy enough" for most of the traditionally male sports in which my parents enrolled him. He felt awkward and embarrassed playing baseball and football and practicing karate, so he stopped participating in sports altogether. Later in life he regretted that; he wished that he had pursued athletics until he found something that felt right. He encouraged me to not let C.J. give up on sports. C.J. had no interest in resurrecting his baseball or soccer careers, he argued that it was too cold to bother with swim lessons (because sometimes it dips below seventy degrees during Orange County's harsh winters), and he was bored with taking gymnastics. I told him that he had to pick some lesson or class that required him to move his body.

"What sport do you want to try next?" I asked.

"Dance!"

I'd had a feeling that the day was coming when my son would become a dancer.

"Hi, I'd like to see if there is availability in the Saturday-morning ballet/tap combo class," I said to the girl at the front desk of our local South Orange County youth gym. It's a converted warehouse where a child can learn to play soccer, swim, cheerlead, take gymnastics, learn aerial arts on silks, practice parkour, attend preschool, have a birthday party, and do just about anything else that will keep business booming for the owners and cater to the OC übermoms who pilot the blacked-out Escalades that are lined up in a neat row out front.

"How old is your daughter?" the front-desk girl asked while scanning her computer screen.

"I don't have a daughter," I said and stared at her. It took her a while to realize that I had a boy who wanted to dance.

"Oh, I'm so sorry. We don't have a tap/ballet combo class for boys," she replied sympathetically, sticking out her bottom lip and tilting her head to the side.

It's the story of my life.

"Okay. Well. Is there room in your Saturday class?" I asked.

"Yeah, does he want to be in there with girls?"

"He'd love nothing more," I said.

There was, in fact, room for C.J. in the class. He was going to die.

We headed to Payless ShoeSource to buy some tap shoes. C.J. could not control himself. When he saw those shiny, patent-leather shoes that made loud noise, with huge black bows on top, he was nearly embarrassed by his own excitement. He held them and rubbed them for a long time before he even thought of putting them on his feet.

"Those are girls' tap shoes. The boys' tap shoes look like this," the Payless ShoeSource salesgirl with crunchy moussed hair said, bending over and exposing her crack while showing us what boys' tap shoes look like. The boys' shoes were not shiny. They were dull black with boring lace-ups, no Mary Jane–like cutouts on top.

"I want the girl ones," C.J. said to me quickly with a look of concern.

"I know you do," I said, ignoring Payless Girl's reaction. When it comes to shoes, we know what we like. We had this handled, thank you very much.

The following Saturday, I awoke to a noise I was not familiar with. It wasn't the house alarm. It wasn't a video game. It wasn't an alarm clock. It wasn't my phone. I threw on my robe and stumbled down the stairs, trying to pry my dry eyes open and brushing my bed head out of my face. The noise got louder. It wasn't even 7:00 a.m.

"Mommy! Good morning! Guess what today is?! My dance class starts today!" C.J. said as he tap-danced in his shoes across our kitchen tile, giving Gregory Hines a run for his money. I made coffee and wondered how I was going to make two hours fly by.

Finally it was time to get dressed. I had been dreading this.

"Where's my dance outfit?" C.J. asked, as if I had been working on a sequined Lycra-and-organdy number in my free time.

"You can just wear workout shorts and a T-shirt," I said.

"No, I can't! I need a tutu!"

Of course he did.

The final ensemble: the tights from his Monster High Frankie Stein Halloween costume, which are green with fake scars and stitches on them, blue Nike athletic shorts, a purple tutu from his dress-up collection, a purple T-shirt, and black socks with skeletons on them. He gazed in the mirror and thought he looked perfect, like the dancer that lived in his soul.

As we walked through the parking lot, through the gym, and up to the second-floor dance studio, it was obvious that not everyone thought C.J. looked as perfect as he thought.

We met his teacher, Miss Rachel. Sometimes you can tell that a person is sweet, nice, and good the moment you meet them. Miss Rachel is one of those people. She has a dancer's body and one dozen freckles sprinkled across her nose like tiny stars. She smiled like she meant it.

I introduced her to C.J. and let her know that we needed to borrow ballet shoes. She showed us to the lost and found.

"I get to wear those?!" C.J. said, smiling.

"Yup."

"ALL OF THEM?!" he squealed, looking at the tub of about a hundred pink lost-and-found ballet shoes.

"No, silly, just two. You only have two feet."

"Ahhhh, maaaaaaaaan." If only he were a centipede.

I returned C.J. to Miss Rachel's class and walked him just inside the door. A little girl pointed.

"Look at that boy!" she laughed and pointed for the other girls to see. The little ballerinas giggled.

C.J. self-consciously found a place on the mat and got ready to stretch. I explained to Miss Rachel that C.J. is gender non-conforming, and she smiled like she knew what it meant. I think the tutu pretty much tipped her off to the fact that C.J. isn't your average boy.

I walked to the area where the parents sat and watched their tiny dancers. I looked at the sets of eyes staring at me as I found a seat. They were watching the new mom who had just brought her son to an all-girls dance class, which had never seen a boy before. And he was wearing a tutu and pink ballet shoes.

I hate being the new mom. I sat down on one of the benches outside the dance studio by myself, looking through the one-way mirror at my son transforming into a dancer.

A mother and daughter came running up to the benches and dropped their bags next me. They were late. The mother started to hastily change her daughter out of her light-up sneakers and into her ballet shoes. As the little girl held on to the bench for balance, she caught sight of C.J.

"Look at the new girl! Why is her hair so short?" she asked loudly.

The mother looked up.

"I don't know, honey. Some girls just like to have their hair really short like a boy," she replied.

"That's my son," I said quietly to the mother. Her face turned fifteen shades of crimson. The mother hurried her daughter into the studio and did not return to her seat next to me. It's okay; I'm used to being avoided. It happens a lot when people see a little boy playing with "girl toys," wearing "girl clothes," or doing something "girly." People avoid things that make them feel uncomfortable or awkward, and we make them feel that way.

But I didn't care at that point because my eyes were glued to C.J. I had never seen him happier, more focused. Finally, he was a dancer. My heart was melting, yet again, for my sweet gender-nonconforming boy.

After the break, during which the kids metamorphosed from ballet dancers into tap dancers with a simple change of shoes, one of the other mothers had no choice but to sit next to me. I decided to get friendly.

"How old is your daughter?" I asked, startling her.

"She's five. How old is your . . . little . . . guy?" she asked, nervously gripping her Starbucks cup for safety. Is a boy in a tutu and ballet shoes in an all-girls dance class still a boy?

"He's going to be five next month," I said with a smile. Apparently there was nothing else to talk about. A mom behind me tapped my shoulder.

"I think it's so great that your son's taking dance. My little girl in there has a twin brother, and I never even thought to ask him if he wanted to try it," she said.

"Thanks." I smiled sincerely.

An advanced adult ballet class started in the studio next door. I was watching the graceful grown ballerinas. A man entered the adult class late. He set his bags down and stripped down to skintight black leggings and a tight, deep V-neck. He found a place on the bar. I watched him move; he was better than every woman in the room.

Before dismissal, everyone in C.J.'s class was given a coloring sheet featuring Hello Kitty as a ballerina as a reward for their hard work. Miss Rachel asked if that was okay for C.J. I assured her that it was right up his alley.

C.J. and I took a few minutes to watch the adults dance next door. C.J. was enraptured.

"Do you see the boy dancing?" I asked, leaning down to his level and pointing as he spotted him.

"Wooooooooow," he said slowly. Oh yeah. He saw him. "Mommy, he's better than the girls. I want to be like that."

"You can be," I said.

In the car on the way home, I asked C.J. if he'd liked dance class.

"I totally loved it!"

The next class couldn't come soon enough. C.J. raced me to Miss Rachel. He was a man, in tights, on a mission. Like a superhero, but different.

"Miss Rachel, today I'm gonna wear my skirt again to class. Can you please tell the girls not to make fun of me?" he said in speech so clear and premeditated that I couldn't believe it had come out of his mouth.

"Oh, sweetie, sure," Miss Rachel said, looking loving and concerned.

I couldn't say anything; there was a lump in my throat. I'd had no idea that he had planned on making that request of Miss Rachel. Matt walked up the stairs then to watch some of C.J.'s moves.

Class started and C.J. was crab-walking across the wood floor.

"We need to work on getting his butt up during the crab walk," Matt said softly. If C.J. had been playing T-ball, he'd have been taking similar mental notes, thinking of ways to help C.J. improve. I love this man for being passionate and interested in the things that speak to C.J.—"gender traditional" or not. I don't tell him enough that it takes a big man to lovingly father a girly boy. He's proof that a bully can be reformed.

"Are boy ballerinas called 'ballerinos'?" Matt interrupted my thoughts. I laughed.

Matt and I took turns watching Chase practice parkour in the main gym downstairs. We were afraid to leave C.J. upstairs alone by himself and afraid of what the other parents might gossip about when we weren't around. We know we shouldn't care, but sometimes we still do. We're all a work in progress all the time.

Class was ending and it was time for coloring sheets. Miss Rachel brought out two options to choose from: SpongeBob SquarePants and Princess Jasmine. Options. Options are good. C.J. went straight for Princess Jasmine. Miss Rachel smiled at me and later acknowledged that with a boy in the class she felt like she should have a "boy" coloring sheet to choose and, even better, that she had never considered that one of the girls might want a "boy" coloring sheet. She turned and walked away, and I read the back of her shirt.

"Wherever you go, go with all your heart."

I grabbed C.J.'s little hand and his tutu and his tap shoes and we went, with all our heart.

Chapter 32

FOR HIS FIFTH BIRTHDAY, C.J wanted a party. A big party. Since his fourth birthday at Disneyland, he had been mentally planning his next birthday party, at which he would be the star for a day in front of an audience larger than his immediate family. As always, the world was his stage, and he wanted to be the lead with a green room filled with his favorite things: hair to brush, Arnold Palmers to drink, and malted milk balls to get chocolate-wasted on.

Again Matt and I struggled with the guest list. If inviting every classmate and their family would put our family at risk of unnecessary hurt feelings, then we weren't about to do it. We had to believe that we were supposed to please our child on his birthday, not every child in his class. We couldn't care about the feelings of others to the extent that we would expose our son to something unfavorable.

We asked C.J. whom he wanted to invite to his party. He named the children he had grown up with, the neighborhood kids, and four girls from his class. We knew most of them well and vice versa. Most of them knew to expect that C.J. would do something flamboyant at his party. He might be wearing an article of girl clothing. The families of the girls he played with at school might be in for a few surprises, and they might have reactions. We had to be okay with that. Love us or leave us, but if you are going to leave us, please do so quietly.

C.J. begged for a party at the local indoor inflatable party zone. That is really fancy talk for a warehouse filled with bounce houses. I liked the bounce-house party idea because it was mostly gender neutral. We did get to bring our own plates and napkins for cake, so off to Party City we went. The birthday party supplies were divided into blue and pink aisles.

"Let's find my aisles," C.J. said as he walked purposefully to the pink aisles, taking large steps and swinging his arms dramatically to imply that he meant business. It was such a tough decision: Hello Kitty, Tinker Bell, Disney Princesses, Little Mermaid. All were given careful consideration. Smurfette was the first runner up, with Monster High taking the win.

Chase wanted to wander the store to see what theme he might want for his birthday, three months later. As we accompanied Chase down the blue aisles, I pointed out some options to C.J.

"How about Hot Wheels?" I said.

"Ewwwww, noooooo," he said, skipping along.

"How about *Star Wars*?"

"Gross," he said, stopping in his tracks to give me a disgusted look.

"How about Diego?" I asked with a smile.

"How about no way!" he said, putting his hands on his hips.

"Mom, you know he doesn't want a boy party," Chase scolded me.

"I'm just making sure he knows all of his options," I replied.

"Well, don't do that; it's mean," Chase told me. I smiled at my older son, who was getting more and more protective of his little brother's gender-nonconforming ways.

A few days later I visited the bounce-house warehouse to pay for the party and scope things out. It all seemed gender neutral and safe for the masses.

"Do you do anything based on gender?" I asked the manager as I was getting ready to leave. "I mean, is there anything that you do specifically by gender or in any way treat the birthday child differently based on gender? Something that you do only for girls or do only for boys?"

Sometimes I even confuse myself.

The woman gave me an odd look and thought and thought and thought before saying, "No, I don't think so."

"Okay, great, because I have a little boy who likes girl stuff and I don't want any part of the party separated by gender," I informed her, hoping that she would make a note of it somewhere in our file. Then I wondered what she would write besides "WARNING: This mom is crazy!"

I can't care what the bounce-house lady thinks. I've learned that I have to ask those kinds of questions; I have to ask them ahead of time, and I usually try to do so without C.J. or Chase within earshot. I especially have to address the issue when it's C.J.'s birthday. It's too important of a day for gender issues to ruin his happiness.

The day before C.J.'s birthday, at 2:35 p.m., the school bell rang, indicating that another day had come to an end for Chase. He hopped into the car. My sweet and sweaty third-grader.

"I need to go shopping. Can you take me to Target?" he said.

"Me too, I need to go shopping too! I wanna go to Target. I love Target!" C.J. yelled from the backseat.

"What do you need from Target?" I asked Chase, ignoring C.J.

"I haven't gotten C.J. a birthday present and his birthday is tomorrow," he said.

Like I needed one more errand to run. I had already been to the grocery store, the toy store, the hardware store, and the party-supply store. I still had to get home to make cupcakes, wrap presents, and prepare the supplies for C.J.'s class party the following day. The big birthday bash was only four days away and had its own to-do list that hadn't even been written yet.

But I agreed to take him to Target because it was so kind of him to even think about getting C.J. a gift. I had a gift for him to give his brother, which I was going to show him that night. But I liked where his head and heart were at. I liked the initiative.

A few hours later, C.J. was busy playing in his room. His dolls were having an argument. They were throwing around phrases like "Oh, snap!" and "Okay, girlfriend?" The more sassily and loudly his dolls speak to one another, the more oblivious he is to the outside world, so I knew he wouldn't notice our departure.

"Do you have your money?" I asked Chase, though I wasn't serious.

"Yeah," he said to my surprise.

"Where'd you get money?" I asked, knowing that he had just blown his last twenty bucks on an online game.

"I helped Pa in the yard this weekend and he paid me ten dollars; I want to use that. I'm going to spend eight dollars on a gift and two dollars on a card."

My heart melted; he even had an estimated budget.

We got to Target and he headed straight to the toy department, directly to the pink aisles, precisely to the Monster High section. He weighed his options and his budget. He did it carefully. Ultimately, he decided on the Monster High Fashion Sketch Book. It was five dollars.

"Now I need to get him a card," he said.

As we were walking to the greeting-card section, he looked at the Monster High ghouls (girls) on the front of the sketchbook and looked at me.

"If the cashier asks, I'm going to tell her that this is for my sister," he said with some serious thought, as if he were warning me politely not to correct him in front of the Target crew member.

"Okay," I said, sad that my eight-year-old son, who was doing such a heartfelt and sincere thing, needed to worry about what the cashier might think or say. These are things that Matt and I have grown used to, numbingly so. But for him, there was still thought that needed to go into navigating a world so firmly rooted in traditional gender norms.

"Ah, here are the girl cards. I need a girl card that plays music. He is going to love it," he said, perusing the racks.

The lady shopping for cards next to us heard his use of pronouns and shot us a quick look. I've gotten really good at ignoring people.

After a good five minutes of reading and listening to every card that played a song when he opened it, Chase decided on one that was more perfect than he knew.

"This. Is. It!" he said, handing the card to me proudly.

It had a picture of a cat on its hind legs dancing on a multi-colored dance floor under a sparkling disco ball.

Front text: Today's your day to get out there and work it . . .
Inside text: Hope your birthday's as fabulous as you are!
Song: Pink's "Get the Party Started"

The cashier ended up not caring whom the present was for, so Chase's prepared answer wasn't needed. That night he wrapped the gift himself and carefully wrote his name on the inside of the card. He taped the envelope shut "just in case."

C.J. opened the present the following evening and loved it.

"C.J., I knew you'd like my present best," Chase said to him as they were brushing their teeth before bed.

"'Cause you know I like girl stuff?" C.J. asked with pink glitter toothpaste running down his chin.

"Yup," Chase said, spitting out his blue toothpaste.

That night as I walked past his room, I could hear Pink singing "Get the Party Started." C.J. had taken the card to bed with him . . . and opened and closed it all night long, getting the party started until midnight.

Finally, the day of C.J.'s big fabulous fifth birthday party arrived. We loaded the party goods into our car and headed to the bounce-house warehouse. We got there just in time for Chase and C.J. to watch the bounce houses come to life, inflating from flat heaps of vinyl into towering structures of silliness. Uncle Michael was just as amused, watching the process with his mouth wide open, standing next to the boys.

"Can I put my dress on now?" C.J. asked.

"Not now, baby, it's going to get in your way when you bounce, and it might rip," I said, setting out coffee for the parents and thinking that a little Baileys to accompany the brew wouldn't have been a bad idea.

Because the plates and napkins we had purchased for post-bounce snacks were Monster High–themed, C.J. wanted to wear his Frankie Stein Halloween costume during the party. But the longer we could keep him in his pumpkin-colored polo with cargo pants the better, for a few reasons. His Frankie costume was getting thrashed and was hard to repair (just ask Nana). If it suffered a major rip during the party, we couldn't be sure of C.J.'s reaction, and we didn't want to take any chances. Another reason to hold off on putting the dress on was that we were meeting some families from school for the first time and we weren't sure how they'd react to meeting a birthday boy who was wearing a dress. If we could at least get the introductions out of the way, Matt and I would feel better.

C.J. got an inflatable crown and wand. He used the wand to beat on Chase during the mandatory safety video the kids had to watch. When the video was over, the kids and Uncle Michael stormed the bounce houses like the bulls of Pamplona. The screams were deafening.

"Mommy, can I put my dress on now?" C.J. asked fifteen minutes into bouncing.

"I'll get it in a minute, baby," I said.

When he asked for the third time, I got the dress from my purse and gave it to him. He exited the bathroom wearing the dress and his cargo pants. He handed me his polo shirt. I didn't look around to see the reactions of strangers; I followed C.J. into a bounce house and bounced with him. He smiled at his skirt flapping with each jump. He smiled at me bouncing. I smiled at the boy having one of his best days ever.

Soon it was time for snacks and cake. C.J. was at the head of the table, next to a little girl named Molly. She was five and one of C.J.'s best friends at school, where they have bonded over their love of Rapunzel and all things pink and purple. Molly has thick, brown, curly hair and a perma-grin. Her happy, round eyes are always alive and looking for fun. She is sweet, the first to notice if one of her friends is hurt or sad. She'll comfort anybody. She reminds me of one of the Precious Moments figurines my grandmother collected when I was young.

It made me pause when I saw her sitting in a seat of honor next to the birthday boy looking troubled. She sat with worried eyes that I hadn't known she owned. Chin in hand, mouth pouty. The kids were all sitting at tables waiting for the cupcakes to be served. I moved in a little closer to eavesdrop.

"I'm so sorry about your present, C.J.," I heard her say.

"Why?" C.J. asked, giving her only half of his attention.

"I'm just so shy about it," she continued. By "shy" she meant embarrassed. Girlfriend had really been giving this issue some serious thought.

"My mommy bought your present while I was at school and she doesn't know that you like girl toys. I thought she knew," Molly said, shaking her head in disappointment.

"Your mommy thinks I like boy toys? Oh my gosh!" C.J. said, giving Molly his full attention upon realizing that they were discussing the birthday gifts he had been waiting 364 days to receive and open.

"I told her before about you liking girl stuff, but then she bought you a SpongeBob book and a *Toy Story* puzzle. I'm so shy," Molly explained, telling C.J. exactly what she had gotten him for his birthday before gift unwrapping even took place. Just then, a cupcake appeared in front of each child.

C.J. got sidetracked with eating his cupcake. Thank goodness, because who knows what he would have said in reply to being informed that he was getting a SpongeBob SquarePants book and a *Toy Story* puzzle. Like all kids his age, he sometimes struggles with things like etiquette, manners, considering the feelings of others, and being gracious. The chances of his saying, "Oh, that's okay, Molly. It's the thought that counts" were slim to none. I know my son; he can be a bit narcissistic.

For example, there was a Beyblade in his last Christmas stocking. He saw it, said with annoyance, "Why would Santa give me a Beyblade?," and promptly hurled it across the room at the Christmas tree. While Uncle Michael tried to hide his elfish laughter behind his mug of spiked eggnog, I crossed the room, retrieved the Beyblade, showed it to C.J., and explained to him that it was a pink Beyblade and that maybe Santa gave it to him so that he could Beyblade battle with his brother and the neighbor kids. Then, and only then, did C.J. consider forgiving Santa.

For the past two and a half gender-nonconforming years, we had been having problems with gifts for C.J. because C.J. likes toys specifically marketed to girls, and sometimes people don't know that or aren't comfortable with giving him "girl toys." And as he gets older, the formerly safe "gender-neutral toys" really annoy him.

Though we've tried to teach him how to graciously accept an unwanted gift, C.J. seems to have an inability to fake happiness and thankfulness when opening a gift he doesn't like. He can be a spitfire. If he doesn't like something, he's going to make it known. Since the Beyblade Christmas, if he opens a "boy toy," we all duck.

Before his party, one mom had asked me what she should buy C.J. for his birthday. I had my response down.

"Anything that you would get for a five-year-old girl," I replied honestly, owning his gender nonconformity much more than I had in the past when asked about gifts for him. I couldn't care about what other people thought; I had to care about my son getting gifts he liked, if he was lucky enough to be getting gifts at all.

"Are you serious?" she asked.

"Yes, and if you aren't comfortable with that, he loves to do crafts or anything artistic."

Three days later, at his birthday party, her child gave C.J. a gender neutral craft kit, which was fine; none of us had to duck. And that book and puzzle Molly gave him? The *Toy Story* puzzle had Jessie and the purple Lotso Bear front and center, so all was right in his world. He gave the SpongeBob book to Chase.

Chapter 33

WHEN C.J. TURNED FIVE, we welcomed a new member into our family. Her name was Chloe and she was C.J.'s invisible friend. She was *not* his imaginary friend, he insisted. Imaginary means made up, not real. Invisible means real, but you can't see her, unless you are C.J. When she first arrived she was seven; two weeks later she was a teenager.

She had long blonde hair, until one day when it turned brown. She was usually wearing a denim skirt and high heels. I'm told that she wore "a *lot*" of lipstick—even to school. If C.J. was shocked by the amount of lipstick she wore, I can only imagine what it looked like. I was worried about her reputation on the playground.

I found C.J. coloring a picture of Cinderella, and his usual staying-inside-the-lines talents went all haywire in the lip area. Cinderella looked as if she had applied a heavy coat of MAC Lady Danger red lipstick and gone to town on Prince Charming. C.J. showed me his artwork, proud as punch.

"Wow, Cinderella's lips are really crazy today!" I said.

"I know. That's how Chloe wears her lipstick," he replied matter-of-factly.

The next day he was coloring a picture of Hello Kitty.

"Oh, C.J., you did such a good job. I like her outfit. Very sassy," I said as he showed me the finished product.

"That's what Chloe is wearing today," he said, referring to Hello Kitty's outfit.

"I thought Chloe only wore jean skirts and high heels," I said in confusion.

"Today she decided to mix it up," he replied, walking away to hang his masterpiece on the refrigerator.

When Chloe was seven, she sat on our car's floorboard between C.J. and Chase as we drove around town. Two weeks later, when she became a teenager, she started traveling on the outside of our car by holding on to the door handle on C.J.'s side of the car. She fluttered and blew alongside our car while trying to maintain her grip. Sometimes she would fly off and C.J. would shout, "Whoopsie!"

We were trying to decide what to listen to on the car stereo one day, and I asked C.J. who Chloe's favorite singer was.

"Ke$ha. Same as me. We love Ke$ha."

Wanting to get the spelling of Chloe's name right for my own sake, I asked C.J. how she spelled it. I gave him the *C* option and the "Khloe Kardashian" option. Turns out she spells it with a *C* so that she and C.J. can have the same initials.

"Are you sure you should be hanging out with a friend who is so much older than you?" I asked when it was just the two—wait, three—of us in the car.

"Yeah, she said that she will be gentle with me 'cause she knows that I'm littler than her," he responded, as if the two of them had already discussed the age difference. My son's invisible friend was a teenage hussy. I would have kept an eye on her if I could have. I was glad to see (figuratively, if not literally) her leave a few months after she entered our lives. She made no grand exit; just suddenly one day she wasn't around anymore.

I mentioned Chloe to C.J.'s pediatrician at C.J.'s five-year checkup. She said that imaginary friends are quite common in childhood and not something to be alarmed about but advised that I keep tabs on the relationship to see if it revealed any of C.J.'s fears, anxieties, or perceptions of the world around him.

We hadn't seen C.J.'s pediatrician in a year, since his last checkup, after which she had sent us to the psychiatrist who informed us that C.J. was not a sexual deviant. I let her know how that appointment had turned out, and she apologized.

"When I was looking through his file in preparation for this appointment, I wondered if his behavior regarding gender was still a concern or if he had grown out of it," the pediatrician said.

"Oh, on the contrary, he's grown more into it, if anything," I said. C.J. was twirling around the room in a hospital gown and knee-high Monster High socks.

I caught her up on our past year and told her about our new therapist. I explained that C.J. is officially, unequivocally gender nonconforming. I had, of course, done my research prior to the appointment and had a list of outcomes I'd like to see realized.

I laid out my list to our pediatrician and, though she didn't have any immediate answers, she worked with us to get them.

"I'm sorry. I know that we are a little high-maintenance," I apologized. I'm always apologizing for our family's being high-maintenance; I can't imagine being low-maintenance at this point. What does that feel like?

"Don't be silly! C.J. is my patient and I need to care for him, the whole him, the best that I can. That's my job," she reassured me. "I've never had a gender-nonconforming patient in my practice before, but I'll do my research and get answers so that I'll be a better doctor for him and future patients like him."

I wanted to see if I could get Darlene's fees reimbursed to us since we were convinced that Kaiser Permanente (our health-insurance company) didn't have a provider who could offer comparable services and expertise and meet our unique needs. The pediatrician tried her hardest to make that happen, but Kaiser found one therapist an hour away in the ghetto of Orange County (yes, we have a few of those) who would see us. I graciously declined. We didn't want to ditch Darlene anyway, but having Kaiser cover her bills would have been nice.

I wanted to know the path we would take if we got to a place where we truly felt that C.J. was transgender. I wanted to know what would be next. Our pediatrician got back to me the next day with the specifics. We would have to be evaluated and establish regular appointments with the ghetto therapist. Then we would be referred to the head pediatric endocrinologist in Kaiser's Southern California region. I got his name and filed it away. An endocrinologist is a doctor who specializes in hormones, among other things. An endocrinologist would work with us to devise a plan of treatment for C.J. It would, most likely, include hormone blockers at the onset of puberty to halt the process and buy us a little more time before larger decisions needed to be made. The larger decisions? Opposite-sex hormones so that C.J. could experience female puberty. The endocrinologist prescribes those as well.

I wanted to know if there was any chance that C.J. was in-tersex; that's the medical term for what was formerly known as hermaphroditism. Was C.J. medically a little of both sexes? Could that be the explanation? It was something Nana Grab Bags suggested we investigate. Darlene said that we should look into it if it would make us feel better, like we had ruled out another possibility, an explanation. But she really didn't think that C.J. was intersex. Darlene was right again. Physi-cally, C.J. is completely and totally all boy.

Around that time, on an episode of his daytime talk show featuring transgender children, Anderson Cooper had on a few experts. One of them was endocrinologist Dr. Lou-ise Greenspan, from Kaiser. An expert on transgender kids who was a doctor with Kaiser? I set out to talk with her, and months later it happened. I had her on the phone and could ask her anything. I was a kid in a transgender, hormone-filled candy shop.

"Most people become aware of gender and the associated body differences at about age three," Dr. Greenspan explained. "That's when they start to understand the differences between the sexes physically and the genders societally. That's when they choose their gender preferences."

"That's exactly what happened in our house with our son," I confirmed. "Close to the age of three he became aware of the gender divide and he chose the girl side. He's five now and identifies as boy, but in terms of gender preferences, they are all girl."

I informed her that he had never asked to transition socially.

"Social transition varies due to family and education settings. I usually see that happening anywhere from age seven or eight to age ten," she said. "It sounds like you have the best-case family support system in place, so the next factor in a situation like yours would be if the school assignment is adequate for transition. Is it safe to transition at school? Would the school support transition?"

"I have no idea, but if transitioning socially were ever to be what he needed, then that would be our priority. If his current school wasn't supportive, I'd find one that was," I said and then asked her about hormone blockers.

"That is an option that, best-case scenario, needs to be discussed prepuberty. Puberty occurs earlier for girls, so with them you start watching for signs of puberty at about age eight. In boys, the earliest you would start looking for puberty is age nine. The hormone blockers are a safe way to wait awhile, and some patients change their mind and decide to go through the puberty that aligns with their sex. Hormones are irreversible. With hormone blockers and hormone replacement, transgender kids, compared to their 'normal' peers, usually end up being on the late end of pubescent development. The earliest that surgical transition can take place is the age of eighteen, and Kaiser performs that surgery for our patients."

I asked her about Kaiser's medical process for transgender patients.

"Kaiser is an ideal model of treatment for transgender patients. We have therapists and medical professionals that are all in network and are, essentially, true colleagues. In my region [Northern California] we have eleven endocrinologists who can help with the medical transitioning process and four who are really, really comfortable with it. In this case, it's a demonstration of the beauty of integrated health care," Dr. Greenspan said.

We talked awhile longer.

"You know, transgender children have the highest rate of suicide. Some medical professionals believe in the 'do no harm' approach to care, but that isn't necessarily the best way to treat these children. Doing nothing may be more harmful. At the same time, it's important not to pigeonhole your child. You need to be right behind him or her, not pushing them or guiding them, but supporting them," she added as our call was approaching its end.

All of the experts I spoke with echoed one another. Support is the key, not steering a child in any one direction but following their lead. Nearly a year after we'd first really considered that C.J. might be transgender, Matt and I felt better emotionally but as if we were in much the same place in our parenting journey. We had no answers about what our future held, but we knew the path we would travel if the answer was yes, if C.J. was transgender, if our son was meant to be our daughter.

Chapter 34

WHILE C.J. WAS TURNING FIVE, totally out as gender non-conforming and more alive than ever, Chase was going through the darkest time of his eight and a half years. He was being teased and harassed almost daily by the class bully, who had seen C.J.'s gender nonconformity in action and, as a result, spread the rumor that C.J. and Chase were gay and used the word "gay" as a slur when talking to or about Chase.

The first time I remember hearing the word "gay" was the summer before fourth grade, when I was attending a Christian summer camp where my brother worked as a camp counselor. One Friday a boy named Jerome, who had always been decent to me, approached me on the playground with a small pack of kids in tow. I was hanging upside down on the monkey bars singing songs and minding my own business.

"Your brother is gay!" Jerome said to me.

I flipped right side up and landed on my feet.

"What?" I asked. I could tell by his tone that we weren't exchanging pleasantries.

"Your brother is gay!" he said again, looking me straight in the eye. Behind him, about a dozen eyes were set on me.

"No, he's not!" I said in rebuttal, summoning up all the courage I could in my state of utter confusion. What the hell did "gay" mean? It didn't sound good; that I could tell. Jerome wouldn't leave me alone about my brother being gay all day. Other kids joined in.

The end-of-the-day bell rang and we were all walking to the parking lot. I saw Jerome and his pack of fourth-grade thugs. They were gaining on me. I was fighting back tears. Before they could circle me, I spun around. I spotted the weakest member of the group, a petite blonde girl named Candace. Jerome again insisted that my brother was gay. "No. He's. Not," I said through gritted teeth. I closed my fist, closed my eyes, and aimed for Candace's face. I grazed her left shoulder and the momentum sent me stumbling. Candace started crying. They had to be tears of shock or fear, because I couldn't possibly have inflicted any pain. She ran to tell on me.

What had I done? I made a beeline for Michael's car to wait for my ride home but was caught by another camp counselor. Candace was cowering behind her. Hot tears formed in my eyes. I was going to be kicked out of church camp; I might be going to jail. I was going to hell for sure.

The counselor sat us both down and asked me why I'd hit Candace.

"They were teasing me," I said. The counselor asked me what they were saying. I wouldn't tell her. I didn't need one more person possibly thinking that my brother was gay, whatever that meant. Candace kept quiet too. We were forced to exchange apologies and told to go straight home.

All the way home I reflected on my first brush with crime and display of physical violence. I couldn't let my parents know that anything out of the ordinary had happened to me that day. I was praying that the camp director wouldn't call my house. I was bargaining with God and the universe. If my parents didn't find out, I'd be good. I'd brush my teeth without being asked. I'd clean my room. I'd make breakfast in bed for the entire family. I'd be nice to Candace, maybe even Jerome. I had all weekend to make amends and put the ugly mess behind me.

One other thing I had to do over the weekend was find out what the word "gay" meant. I couldn't ask my mom, dad, or brother. I knew that. I knew it was a bad word, and I didn't need them asking me where I had heard it.

I don't remember who gave me the answer I was looking for, but when they told me that it meant that two boys loved each other and were boyfriends and French-kissed, I remember thinking, *Well, of course my brother's not gay! He's had girlfriends! I've seen him kiss a girl! He went to prom with a girl!*

Then I was a little disgusted that someone would even think that about him. What had my brother done to make them think that? Jerome wasn't the last person to tease or bully me because of my brother's presumed or confirmed sexuality. As much as I hated it, I always knew that my brother had it worse; I knew he got teased more often and more harshly than I did, so I never complained.

Years later, on the night my brother came out, I thought of Jerome and Candace. All of my bullies had been right. Damn them, they'd known something about me that I hadn't known. I felt like a fool. The bad people were smarter than I was.

More than twenty years after my incident on the playground, Chase's bullying story started. In first grade Steven teased Chase for no real reason we could identify. Sometimes you just don't like another person. And Steven just didn't like Chase. Things got physical near the end of first grade, when Steven pushed Chase down on the blacktop during recess. When first grade ended, we were happy to be done with Steven.

One morning early in the second-grade school year, C.J. and I walked Chase to the blacktop, where the kids line up by classroom number and, once the school bell rings, shuffle toward their classrooms with their teachers at the front of the pack. We arrived early and the teacher wasn't there, so we stood around waiting, trying to wake up. We have never been morning people.

Steven approached us and stared. And stared. And stared. Finally he smirked and ran away. What the hell was he looking at, and what about us was so amusing to him? I had to do a quick scan. We were all out of our pajamas and dressed, zippers were up, noses were boogerless. Check, check, and check. We were officially presentable. Then I saw that C.J. was holding his rather-large-in-comparison-to-his-body *Alice in Wonderland* plush doll. I hadn't finished my checklist! All girl toys hadn't been left in the car. No check. That must have been what that seven-year-old punk smirked at.

Five and a half hours later I picked up Chase from school. His head was down as he climbed into the car. Something was bothering him.

"What's wrong?" I asked.

"Steven was giving me a hard time at school today," he muttered.

"*What?* I can't hear you!" C.J. yelled noisily from the back-seat. He's always in everybody's business.

"What happened?" I asked.

"I'll tell you later," he said, thumb-pointing to C.J. in the backseat to indicate that he didn't want his little brother to hear.

"*What?* Tell me!" C.J. said eagerly, trying to lean forward toward the front seat but being restrained by his seat belt and car seat. I could understand why Chase might want to wait until we got home.

Once we were able to slip away from C.J., Chase told me that Steven, after seeing C.J. with Alice in Wonderland, had approached him and said, "Your brother likes dolls. Your brother is gay!" A few other kids had overheard.

"His brother is gay. Eeewwwwwww!" Steven had said, pointing at Chase and backing up. The kids in the audience started to laugh and back up and run away from Chase. For days nobody would play with him at lunch or recess because Steven started the rumor that his brother was gay, and not the "happy" kind of gay.

"I'm so sorry that that happened to you, honey. Steven is a real jerk," I said in comfort to my son.

"What does 'gay' mean?" he asked me.

That's when I explained homosexuality to my second-grader. I told him that it means that you are a boy who loves a boy or a girl who loves a girl and you want to spend your life with that person instead of being a boy who loves a girl or a girl who loves a boy.

"That's weird," he said.

"Is it weird or different?" I asked.

"I guess it's not weird. It's just different from you and Daddy," he said thoughtfully.

"Yup," I said, watching him think, wondering if Michael and his boyfriend would come up.

We never announced to Chase that Michael was gay, because, we reasoned, we never would have announced if Michael was straight and had sex with women. We figured that we would let it naturally occur to Chase over time. But it never did. Then it got to the point where it would have felt unnatural to explain the whole thing to him in a sit-down conversation. But I also never wanted him to feel deceived, as I had when my brother came out to me.

Once, when Chase was four and Michael was visiting, Chase asked him where his wife was.

"I don't have one," Michael answered.

"Why not?" Chase asked.

"Because I don't want one," Michael answered.

"Me neither," Chase said, looking out the window as we drove along.

Was that the time when we should have told Chase that his uncle is gay? It never feels like the right time to come out.

"So being gay is like loving your best friend and living with them and not wanting to be in love with or live with anybody else," Chase said after I explained what it meant to be gay. He was trying to put it in terms that he could better understand.

"Yes," I said, because if you take sex out of it, that's the truth.

"I want to be gay with my friend Jax," he said. I panicked.

"Okay, well don't go telling Jax or anybody else that just

yet," I said quickly. "Because you may change your mind and you are too young to move out and it's too early for all of that."

"Yeah, you're right." Whew.

Throughout second grade Steven harassed and bullied Chase. They were not in the same class, but because they were in the same grade, they saw each other during recess and lunch. Chase decided he was going to have a talk with Steven.

"How come you don't like me?" Chase asked him.

"I don't know, I just don't," Steven said. Well, at least he was honest, I guess.

"Well, do you think that we can make up and be friends?" Chase suggested.

"We can try," Steven said.

Chase was so happy for a fresh start, then heartbroken that it only lasted for a few weeks. Steven quickly resumed telling their peers that Chase and his brother were gay and that C.J. liked girl stuff. When second grade ended, we were again glad to be done with Steven.

The day before third grade started, we piled into the car and made the end-of-summer pilgrimage to the elementary school, where the class assignments would be listed. Kids ran amok, with bare feet, tans, and fresh haircuts, as their parents scanned class rosters to see who would teach their child for the school year that would start the next day. I skimmed the third-grade lists and saw that Chase would be in Mrs. Riley's class. I'd heard mixed opinions about her. But C.J.'s gender nonconformity has taught me to, in most cases, ignore gossip and uneducated opinions and form my own opinions. If I got an "I told you so" along the way because of it, so be it.

I scanned Mrs. Riley's class roster to see if Chase's best friend, Jax, was in the class. I was running my right index finger down the list of names when it happened. It rolled over Steven's name. My finger went to my lips and my face went hot. Steven was in Chase's class. Crap.

"Who'd I get, Mom?!" Chase asked, bumping into me from behind.

"You got Mrs. Riley!" I said with all of the excitement a parent is supposed to have to amp up the kid and get him/her excited for the next day.

"Cool!" Chase said, mostly because he thinks everything is cool, not because he knew enough about her to think that Mrs. Riley was cool.

We drove home and I called Matt at work to tell him that Chase and Steven would be in class together.

"Well, we'll have to see how it goes. Maybe things will be different this year," Matt said reassuringly.

We talked to Mrs. Riley and warned her about the history between Chase and Steven. We also let her know that a majority of the bullying seemed to be fueled by our younger son's gender nonconformity. She listened, thanked us for letting her know, promised to seat them at desks on opposite sides of the classroom, and said that she would keep an eye on them.

During the first thirty days of third grade, Chase endured daily taunts from Steven and one instance of major bullying. I reported it and was assured that it had "been handled." Steven continued to tease and bully Chase outside of the classroom on a regular basis, most often using hate speech and slurs meant to degrade the LGBTQ community. He constantly questioned both of our sons' gender presentation and future sexuality.

The next month, Chase fell during PE, ripped his jeans, and got a bloody knee. PE was the last subject of the day, and Chase was five minutes later than usual getting to my car at the pickup line. I saw him limping to the car with Steven right behind him saying, "Aw, poor baby, did you hurt your leg? Is your leg broken, crybaby? Why don't you go tell your mommy?"

"The pressure is building inside me and I'm afraid the top is going to pop off," Chase said and started crying once he got into the safety of my car. As I listened, I felt helpless.

I turned my head to the left so that he wouldn't see the tears in my eyes as I drove. When I got home, I sent an e-mail to both Mrs. Riley and Principal Whitaker, reminding them of Steven's bullying behavior during the past two and a half years and outlining in detail the incidents from the first sixty days of the new school year. I reminded Mrs. Riley, and let Mrs. Whitaker know for the first time, that Steven targeted Chase because of his gender-nonconforming little brother. I asked both women to contact me. Principal Whitaker ignored me outright, but Mrs. Riley replied to my e-mail, letting me know that she would "address" the issue with Steven and that she didn't "understand [the situation] to be any more serious than issues other children have with each other in the third grade." The phrase "age-appropriate teasing" was thrown around. I again asked Principal Whitaker to contact me and was again ignored.

During the Thanksgiving and Christmas breaks we got Chase in to see a therapist, his own therapist, because apparently every member of our family needs their own therapist. Steven's bullying was affecting Chase's sleep, appetite, anxiety level, and feelings toward C.J. Chase was experiencing frequent and severe stomachaches. He asked to be transferred to a different school. He started tracking Steven's dates of punishment and figured out a pattern: Chase knew that if he told on Steven, the bullying would cease and he would be "safe" for approximately one to one and a half weeks. Then the insults would continue even more frequently and more aggressively, with Steven calling Chase a "crybaby" for tattling.

From the moment C.J. picked up that Barbie in my bedroom, we had worried about his getting bullied and teased. We ignorantly never guessed that Chase would be teased just as much for his brother's gender nonconformity. We never anticipated that would be the bullying we'd have to deal with first. We didn't expect it, but we probably should have.

In February, on my way to pick up C.J. from pre-K, I walked past the lunch tables where Chase sat among the sea of third-graders. Chase called out to me and waved hello. I waved back to him and smiled. My boy was so sweet.

Because of that wave and greeting, Steven spent days spreading the rumor that I still breastfed Chase. Matt, Chase, and I were mortified by Steven's latest bullying tactics. Out of embarrassment, Chase begged us not to report the incident to Mrs. Riley or Principal Whitaker. We obliged and grew to regret it.

Later that month, Steven called Chase gay in front of a group of their peers because he had screamed in too high a pitch on the playground. One of those boys told a campus supervisor, and Steven's punishment was to sit on a bench for the remainder of that recess. Chase arrived home from school crying, and it took a lot of persuading to get him to return to school the next day.

I wrote an e-mail to Mrs. Riley, Principal Whitaker, and Vice Principal Boone. The e-mail included all of the correspondence I had sent to the school since September. The history was all there.

Mrs. Riley let me know that she had already been made aware of Steven's calling Chase gay. She said that Steven had been given an "immediate consequence" and been "talked to" by an assistant principal. I continued to be told that the boys had no interaction in the classroom and that, because Steven targeted Chase away from the classroom and adult supervision, it was hard to prevent the bullying and know what was really happening. Principal Whitaker and Vice Principal Boone never replied to my e-mail.

Matt and I were feeling just as hopeless and helpless as Chase, but we couldn't let him see that. We worked every day to make sure that Chase felt safe and loved and like we were doing something about the bullying, were taking it very seriously, and were working to protect him no matter what. But we had no idea what to do next. Something had to be done, but what?

Chapter 35

"I WANT TO KILL MYSELF so that all of the fear and anxiety leaves my body. Then I want to be alive again," Chase told Nana Grab Bags at the end of February.

We'd had enough of the bullying. I remembered that a mom from my PFLAG chapter was working as a research assistant on a bullying project at a local university. I reached out to her and she called me right away.

I told her about the entire history of bullying by Steven. She was a wealth of information. She explained that the benching or other immediate consequences being given to Steven were all simply punishments and were doing nothing to teach him about diversity to change his actions and the culture on campus. She told me that our family had legal rights that were being violated. Why didn't I know that? She e-mailed me tons of resources and told me to continue to document everything that was happening with Chase at school. Then she set up a meeting for us with her and the professor she worked under at the university.

Karyl is an assistant professor of women and gender studies at California State University, Fullerton. When we met her for brunch, we were in panic mode. If some change for the better didn't happen soon, we didn't know what Chase would do; our family was in the middle of a crisis. Every night at dinner, when we'd have Chase tell us about the best part of his day and the worst part of his day, Steven was always the worst part of his day. Steven was the worst part of my day too; I just never told Chase.

Karyl is an antibullying superhero. She earned her cape and superpowers while protecting her daughter, who was a high-schooler involved in drama and theater and was upset because her class's production of the musical *Rent* had been canceled because the production was not "high school friendly." After Karyl's daughter expressed her disappointment, three of the school's top athletes posted a video on the school's Facebook page describing in detail how they were going to rape and kill her. They also made homophobic remarks about another student.

The school administration mostly did nothing about the incident, so Karyl went to the American Civil Liberties Union (ACLU), which would do something. It filed a lawsuit against the school and emerged victorious, or as victorious as anybody can emerge in a situation like that.

Karyl went on to create an extended-education course titled Understanding and Addressing Bullying, which is designed to teach educators and school officials more about how to correctly handle bullying related to gender identity, gender presentation, sexual orientation, and perceived sexual orientation. It was the first professional-development curriculum course of its kind for education professionals and was offered by California State University, Fullerton.

Karyl quickly became our advocate and dished out assignments to us. We have never been so thankful for a to-do list in all our lives. Following her advice, I started researching the Department of Education's Title IX and the ACLU of Southern California's Seth Walsh Students' Rights Project.

It took me seven days to get my hands on our school district's official antibullying policy. I could find its stance on the whooping cough vaccine and a list of which district athletic fields had been recently sprayed with pesticide, but I couldn't find information on what the district would do if my son was scared to go to school because Steven had convinced everybody that he was a homosexual, breastfeeding crybaby.

I went to the school's office and requested a copy of the antibullying policy. I was met with blank stares from two office clerks, who, after much deliberation, decided that I should look on the school's website, not the district's website.

"The school website only contains the school's behavior policy and discipline program, not an antibullying policy," I said.

"Jeez, well, then, I don't know," one of the clerks told me.

I went home and called the district's office and requested a copy of the district's antibullying/harassment policy. I was transferred to human resources and employee relations, and then I was hung up on. I called back.

"Hi, I need to know who is the district's Title IX rep," I said to the third person I had been transferred to.

"I don't think we have one" was the answer.

"You're legally required to have one," I replied.

"We are?"

"Yes. I also need a copy of the district's antibullying/harassment policy and haven't been able to locate it," I said.

Phrases like "Title IX" and "antibullying/harassment policy" and "legally required" should have made some sort of alarm go off in the lady's head.

"Do you want me to transfer you to employee relations?" she asked, confused.

"Where would you transfer someone reporting a severe discipline problem and extreme bullying?" I asked.

"Hold on," she said, transferring me to another woman, who took my contact information and promised that someone would get back to me.

I went to the ACLU of Southern California's website and, per Karyl's instructions, looked for information on the Seth Walsh Project, which changed everything. There's comfort in knowing that you aren't crazy and that you have rights.

The Seth Walsh Project was created to "stop the unlawful bullying and harassment in California schools and to create school communities that promote safety and respect for all students. [It] was prompted by the September 2010 suicide of Seth Walsh, a 13-year-old middle school student. . . . Since coming out as gay in the sixth grade, Seth was subjected to severe verbal harassment based on his sexual orientation and refusal to conform to traditional gender stereotypes."

Within the Seth Walsh Project pages of the ACLU of Southern California's website, there was a list of rights that identified—or perceived—LGBTQ students have in the state of California.

"The California Education Code says that schools must

protect students from different kinds of bias, including harassment based on sexual orientation or gender identity. This means that you can't be harassed for being LGBTQ, for people thinking you are LGBTQ or for having friends or family members who are LGBTQ. . . . School administration can't just ignore anti-LGBTQ harassment or discrimination of students."

I called the Seth Walsh Students' Rights Project hotline and left a message. A very nice young man got back to me promptly and listened patiently as I gave him the long history between Steven and Chase. He determined that the school and district were in violation of state laws, including the California Education Code. Furthermore, Chase's civil rights were being violated. He offered to send a letter to the school and the district. He told me that I needed to fill out a Uniform Complaint Procedure Discrimination/Harassment Complaint Reporting Form from the ACLU and Department of Education and submit it to our district. He showed me exactly where the form was located online. He said that the ACLU could get as involved as I wanted it to.

I talked to Matt. We were both relieved that we had a legitimate case that could force change so that Chase could be done with Steven once and for all. We decided that our goal was to have Steven transferred to another classroom. We also decided that we wanted to try to work with the school and district without the involvement of the ACLU. If we gave it a go and got nowhere, we'd call the ACLU in right away. That decision was made out of fear of retribution. If we didn't move, we had thirteen more school years in the district, and we'd like those to go as smoothly as possible. We wanted to give the school and district one more chance to make things right.

I stayed up ridiculously late completing the Uniform Complaint Procedure Discrimination/Harassment Complaint Reporting Form and an accompanying form I received from the district. As I did so, Matt kept peering over my shoulder at the computer.

"Good job, Mama," he said. He has always been there with me every step of whatever journey I take.

I completed the forms and sent them to Karyl for her to review, and I called the school office to schedule a meeting with Vice Principal Boone.

"You can just e-mail him," the office clerk told me over the phone.

"I want to schedule an in-person meeting," I said.

"Hold on," she said to me. I could hear her talking to the other office clerk. "Bonnie, somebody wants to schedule a meeting with Mr. Boone. Do we do that? I think it's a parent."

"We're going to have to call you back," she said, talking to me again. "We don't know how to do that."

"Do you have access to his calendar?" I asked.

"I don't think so," she said. *These people would be eaten alive in the business world,* I thought. Give me one week in the school or district office and I could get the place running. I could teach people to view other people's calendars, schedule meetings, post pertinent documents in the appropriate places, transfer calls, and e-mail files. I could blow their minds.

Mr. Boone called me back the next day and put Matt and me on his calendar for a few days later. I didn't tell him that

Karyl would be joining us. I thought about it, but the truth was, I didn't feel like I owed it to him to prepare him for the force of nature that Karyl is. I wanted him to be shocked.

I got myself really familiar with Title IX of the Education Amendments of 1972. I devoured a 2010 letter about Title IX issued by the United States Department of Education and signed by the assistant secretary for civil rights.

> Bullying fosters a climate of fear and disrespect that can seriously impair the physical and psychological health of its victims and create conditions that negatively affect learning, thereby undermining the ability of students to achieve their full potential. The movement to adopt anti-bullying policies reflects schools' appreciation of their important responsibility to maintain a safe learning environment for all students. . . . Some student misconduct that falls under a school's anti-bullying policy also may trigger responsibilities under one or more of the federal anti-discrimination laws enforced by the Department of Education's Office for Civil Rights. . . . School districts may violate these civil rights statutes and the Department's implementing regulations when peer harassment based on race, color, national origin, sex or disability is sufficiently serious that it creates a hostile environment and such harassment is encouraged, tolerated, not adequately addressed or ignored by school employees. . . . A school is responsible for addressing harassment incidents about which it knows or reasonably should have known.

There is a whole section on gender-based harassment. Title IX "prohibits gender-based harassment, which may include acts of verbal, nonverbal, or physical aggression, intimidation, or hostility based on sex or sex-stereotyping. Thus, it can be sex discrimination if students are harassed either for exhibiting what is perceived as a stereotypical characteristic for their sex, or for failing to conform to stereotypical notions of masculinity and femininity. Title IX also prohibits sexual harassment and gender-based harassment of all students, regardless of the actual or perceived sexual orientation or gender identity of the harasser or target."

> Title IX does protect all students, including lesbian, gay, bisexual, and transgender (LGBT) students, from sex discrimination. . . . The fact that the harassment includes anti-LGBT comments or is partly based on the target's actual or perceived sexual orientation does not relieve a school of its obligation under Title IX to investigate and remedy overlapping sexual harassment or gender-based harassment. . . . The school [has] an obligation to take immediate and effective action to eliminate the hostile environment.

At the end of the first week of March, after the dismissal bell rang at school, Steven and Chase collected their backpacks from outside of their classroom and Steven stood in front of Chase, blocking his path and not letting him pass. It was another one of Steven's regular tactics. Chase pushed Steven. It was the first time Chase had laid his hands on Steven.

"Knock it off, Steven, I'm sick of you bullying me!" he said to his tormentor.

"What, are you gonna cry about it, crybaby?" Steven taunted.

"Do you see me crying?" Chase asked.

"Yeah, I do!" Steven lied.

"Get your backpack and get out of here," Chase said before stepping around Steven and arriving at my car upset, again. When we got home, Chase hid under the dining room table and couldn't be coaxed out. He said he was sick of Mrs. Riley, Principal Whitaker, and Vice Principal Boone doing nothing to protect him at school or to get Steven to leave him alone.

I got on the floor and talked to Chase and promised, for real, that something drastic would be done this time.

The next morning Matt and I met Karyl in the front of the school by the flagpole. We thanked her with our whole hearts for being there with us, and we walked together into Vice Principal Boone's office.

He looked confused and overwhelmed. I found some small amount of joy in that. I presented him with a file on our issue that I had created for the school and let him know that I had another copy for the district, which I would deliver to the district's Title IX rep immediately following our meeting.

I pulled out our copy of the file and walked Vice Principal Boone through the contents, in which I detailed every major incident of bullying, talked about the day-to-day harassment, and emphasized that requests for communication with school administration had gone unanswered. I stressed that this was a pattern of misconduct, not just a bunch of separate incidents. I outlined how we had asked Chase's teacher, principal, and vice principal to improve the school climate and implement anti-bullying efforts to help us ensure that our son felt safe at school and that the requests had been ignored and/or dismissed by the principal and vice principal. I alleged that the school administration had not adequately responded to Steven's persistent harassment of Chase, especially since Steven's behaviors were based on the perceived sexual orientation and gender identity of Chase and his younger brother.

Karyl took over on our behalf and informed Vice Principal Boone that the school and, therefore, the district were in violation of the California Department of Education's policies and procedures put in place to cease unlawful discrimination against protected groups. She said that in her research she had found the school not to be in compliance with state and federal education codes (such as Title IX), and she gave Vice Principal Boone several detailed actionable measures that would help reset the campus culture in light of the events surrounding Steven and Chase and the language of homophobia that was already present on campus.

She formally recommended that the school follow its own discipline/behavior-management policy and suspend Steven for at least one day as soon as possible, which should have happened some time ago, after the first incident was reported. This would be key to sending Chase, and the other students who had witnessed the homophobic bullying, the message that their right to a safe learning environment would be protected by the administration in accordance with state and federal laws.

She expressed our wish to have Steven moved permanently out of Chase's class. Having to endure physiological stress on a daily basis for years, as Chase had, is unacceptable for any age or grade level and is a direct violation of the California safe schools laws.

She requested that the school comply with Title IX by

posting the school's "Uniform Complaint Form" on the school's website and comply with California Title IX and safe-schools laws by identifying who the district's Title IX officer was and including that information on the school's website. School staff should also know who this important resource person is and how to contact her/him. The school should also comply with California Title IX and safe-schools laws by clearly posting the school's antiharassment/antibullying policy around the campus. This should be in a form that was easily understood by all students.

Next Karyl focused on Steven and his needs. Yes, the kid had needs too; during our first meeting with her, she helped us see that. As much as the school and the district were doing a disservice to Chase and our family, they were doing the same to Steven and his family. If Steven was acting like this in first, second, and third grade, what kind of behavior would he be displaying in middle school and high school? We couldn't let prejudice breed prejudice. We couldn't hate Steven because he hated us. He needed help too.

So we didn't hesitate when giving Karyl the okay to ask the school to provide or refer Steven and his family to counseling services, noting that his age-inappropriate language and behavior indicated that he truly was a child at risk. She provided Vice Principal Boone with research on bullying as a predictive behavior of adult violence.

The meeting slowly came to an end, and Vice Principal Boone walked us out, looking even more confused and overwhelmed than he had an hour earlier when we'd entered his office. Matt and I walked out to the parking lot with Karyl. We thanked her again, sincerely and wholeheartedly.

Our official complaints were reviewed and investigated by a district representative—who was Mrs. Whitaker; I still don't understand how a person can be charged with fairly investigating claims made against her. We met with Mrs. Whitaker to learn her/the district's formal findings. In short, Steven admitted to pretty much all of his bullying behavior. We were shocked. The school's administration and the district owned up to nothing. The adults in the situation owned up to less than the child. Sad.

Steven was immediately removed from Chase's class and would never be placed in his class again. He was also banned from having any contact with Chase, and all staff and faculty at the school were made aware of the situation and charged with ensuring that Steven stayed away from Chase. Matt and I considered it a victory. So did Karyl. Most important, so did Chase. He felt safe at school again, and we were happy to be done with Steven once and for all.

Chapter 36

FINALLY IT WAS THE LAST week of school. The South Orange County Mommy Mafia was out in full force, giving each day a theme and a party and a sense of panic that had me constantly feeling as if I were forgetting some important detail. They scuttled about campus in their Lululemon yoga pants, clutching their stainless-steel commuter mugs filled with the organic coffee they'd picked up at Trader Joe's over the weekend while they were loading up on supplies for the class ice-cream social, board-game mixer, pizza party, beach-blanket barbecue, popcorn-and-movie midday madness, and bubble-blowing farewell ceremony. I watched them all from the comfort of my dirty car, wearing my work pants that give me a severe muffin top and drinking yesterday's coffee, which I had managed to burn when I'd reheated it in the microwave.

I remember when I was in school and there was only one celebration; it was called the final bell ringing, marking the start of summer. That was the official party, the bell; it lasted five seconds.

I spent no less than seven days meeting the demands of the mafia and trying to keep up with my two sons and the days' many themes and parties so that I didn't seem like a clueless, uncaring, uninvolved mom. I have to admit, I burst out in insane laughter when one of the boys' room moms sent an e-mail reminding us that there was a party the next day and she still needed "multiple parents to supply wet, squirtable toppings."

Excuse me? File that between "Room Mom Epic Fail" and "I've Got Your Wet Toppings Right Here." I was thankful for tiny moments of hilarity in an otherwise hectic week.

But while I was feeling overwhelmed by the end-of-the-year festivities, give C.J. a theme and he will run with it. The last week of school had him running for five days straight. For C.J., Monday was pirate day.

"C.J., do you want to dress like a pirate for school today?" I asked.

"No, that's not fun," he said with a look of disappointment.

He wasn't quite as glum hours later when I picked him up from school and he was wearing the awesome pirate hat he'd made in class. He had customized his Jolly Roger, complete with rainbow wig and purple grill.

Another day that week was sports day.

"What do you want to wear for sports day? You can wear your baseball uniform or your soccer uniform or . . ."

"I want to be a cheerleader!" C.J. interrupted. "I already have my uniform, you know the pink one with glitter?"

Oh, I knew which one he was talking about: the one I'd bought for him after he'd dislocated his elbow while riding his bike a few months earlier. It was two sizes too small, ripped, and stained. Nana Grab Bags had worked her sewing magic on it a few times, but you can only do so much when working with a fifteen-dollar, imitation-satin frock.

"Baby, that uniform is too small and too worn out to wear to school," I said honestly. It was a tattered mess.

"Okaaaaaay, I guess I'll wear my baseball uniform," he said, lacking enthusiasm. "When's pajama day?"

"Friday."

"That will be *my* day. I'm going to wear my *Little Mermaid* jammies to school," he declared.

I looked at Matt. Were we really going to let our son wear girls' pajamas to school? Considering he doesn't own a pair of boys' pajamas, either our options were limited or I needed to go shopping—not that I ever mind a good excuse to go shopping.

"Are you cool with him wearing girl pajamas to school?" I asked Matt later that night, away from the boys.

"Yeah, I don't care. School's almost over," he said.

"I agree."

It had been a tough school year dealing with gender issues, and we felt as if we were just doing whatever it took to get through the final days of the school year and to the safety of summer.

I e-mailed C.J.'s teacher, Mrs. Meyer, to warn her that C.J. would be wearing his three-piece deluxe *Little Mermaid* pajama set, which we recently purchased on sale at the Disney Store, to school on Friday. Pants with fish-scale tail design, white top with Ariel on it, and optional layered skirt, which C.J. has never considered optional; to him, it's mandatory.

She replied the next day before noon that C.J. was welcome to wear anything he was comfortable in.

I picked C.J. up from school. He sat in his booster seat wearing his baseball uniform.

"Mommy, today Mrs. Meyer told me that I could wear my *Little Mermaid* jammies to school for pajama day. She said I could wear whatever makes me comfortable and that she'll tell the kids not to make fun of me. She said that people will like me no matter what," he said.

"Mrs. Meyer is right. She's a good teacher."

"So, can I wear my *Little Mermaid* jammies to school tomorrow?"

"No, tomorrow is crazy-hair day."

"What?!! I *love* crazy-hair day!!!!"

"That's odd—you've never had a crazy-hair day before," I said, smiling at C.J. in the rearview mirror as I drove.

"I know, but I know I'm just going to love it."

Finally it was Friday, pajama day. C.J. had allowed me to wash his favorite *Little Mermaid* pajamas. He put them on and then sprayed some of my Victoria's Secret body mist on himself. He was ready.

Then we got to school and he didn't want to get out of the car.

"What if somebody sees me?" he asked in worry.

"They'll see your fabulous *Little Mermaid* pajamas," I said. "If you want to change, I have a pair of your brother's old pajamas that you can wear instead."

"No, I'm good."

He sat quietly looking out the window for a minute or two. I could tell he was gathering his courage. His little chest took a deep breath and he opened the car door. He had made his own decision, and I walked behind him to class. I had his back every step of the way.

We got some looks; I'm not going to lie. Then his friend Isabella walked up to him.

"C.J., you look soooooo pretty in your *Little Mermaid* pajamas," she said with admiration and a smile.

"Thank you," C.J. said shyly. It was the highlight of his day.

Mrs. Meyer took the pajamaed kids into her classroom and sat them down. She explained that it was pajama day and everybody was wearing what they were comfortable in, that people are comfortable in different kinds of pajamas and that's okay. She reminded them that teasing was not okay on pajama day or any other day. C.J. got lots of looks that day, a few compliments, but no teasing remarks.

C.J.'s graduation from prekindergarten was overflowing with all of the pomp and circumstance you'd expect to accompany the age-old right of passage marking the end of preschool (with its wait lists and tuition higher than a car payment) and the start of elementary school.

C.J.'s last days of the school year had been so themed that Walt Disney might have learned a thing or two. The culmination was a Hawaiian-themed graduation ceremony featuring a multisong performance by the graduates, the crossing of the stage to accept diplomas, and a potluck barbecue that offered no less than three different types of salad.

When C.J. learned that graduation was a themed event, he immediately threw himself into planning his outfit. He went searching through his dress-up bins looking for his grass skirt, the one I'd brought back from Hawaii the summer before. He couldn't find it. Maybe because it had morphed into a tangled, grassy mess with at least one piece of gum in it and ended up in the trash. Maybe.

"But I *need* a grass skirt for my Hawaii graduation. I *need* to look like a hula girl," C.J. informed me.

I, in turn, e-mailed Mrs. Meyer once again, to let her know that my son would be wearing at least some portion of a hula-girl getup to the graduation ceremony. We were going out of pre-K with a bang.

I let him look for the long-gone grass skirt for two days, because it kept him busy and because I would never admit to having purged it.

Mrs. Meyer replied to my hi-my-son-wants-to-wear-a-skirt-to-graduation e-mail. She let me know that a few of the girls in class planned on wearing grass skirts to graduation and that C.J. should feel free to do the same if he wanted to.

We set off to Party City to replace the lost/trashed/missing grass skirt. As luck would have it, workers were setting up three aisles of luau party supplies, which would remain intact until they were converted to the costume aisles for Halloween.

C.J. had his pick of the litter. There were grass skirts in a variety of colors: rainbow, pink, orange, green, brown, natural, blue, and yellow. I saw the rainbow-colored skirt and knew that it would be the one C.J. would pick, but I stood there and let him go through the decision-making process. He couldn't decide and he couldn't decide and he couldn't decide.

"I thought you'd want the rainbow one for sure," I said.

"I think I want the blue one," he said after some more consideration.

I was speechless. C.J. had never, ever, picked a blue anything.

I was afraid he was picking it because, if he was going to wear a skirt in front of all of his classmates and their families, he felt that it would be safer to wear a boy-colored one.

"Baby, it's up to you if you want to wear a grass skirt or not. It's your choice. And you can pick any color you want," I reminded him.

"I want the blue one. I like the blue one."

"Are you sure? Once we buy it, that's it. There's no changing your mind about the color," I said.

"I'm sure. I want the blue skirt."

"All right, then, let's go pay for it."

We got home and he immediately put the skirt on. He moved throughout the house all evening very carefully, so that he wouldn't get his grass tangled. Before he went to bed that night, he laid out his outfit for the next day's graduation ceremony. Light-blue-and-cream plaid shirt, khaki shorts, brown sandals, blue grass skirt, rainbow lei, and a fake corsage for each wrist—one blue and one red. He put extra leave-in conditioner in his hair because he was convinced that the berry-smelling spray makes his hair grow longer and prettier faster and he was on a mission to have it "long like a girl" in time for kindergarten in September. He got in bed early but didn't fall asleep until after 11:00 p.m. Tomorrow he would be a graduate.

The next day, as we walked to his classroom, C.J. was beaming. He was the only graduate who had worn a grass skirt; none of the girls in class had—as they'd said they would—worn one. I was worried that C.J. would want to take his skirt off, that he wouldn't want to be the only one wearing one. On the contrary, being the only one in a grass skirt and making his girl friends a little envious made him feel even more fabulous. As far as he was concerned, he was the star of the graduation.

"I like your hula-girl skirt, C.J.," Molly said. "My mom wouldn't let me wear mine. You're lucky your mom let you wear yours."

"I know," C.J. said.

As I watched C.J. on the stage, I was proud as could be.

"Look at the little boy in the skirt!" a woman said behind me, and I heard a few laughs.

Yep, that was my son, up on the stage in a skirt, singing "I'll Be Going to Kindergarten Next Year" to the tune of "She'll Be Coming 'Round the Mountain." People could laugh and point all they wanted. I didn't care. Not today.

After the graduation ceremony, I was in line for the potluck lunch when Mrs. Meyer approached me.

"I just wanted to say that it was such a pleasure having C.J. in my class this year," she said.

"Oh my gosh, are you kidding me? I was going to thank you for being so amazing. I know that we are high-maintenance and you've never taught a kid like C.J., and you taught him with an open mind and an open heart, and that's all we ask for," I gushed.

"Well, I really enjoyed C.J. He allowed me to learn something new. I love learning new things. And I've watched him grow so much emotionally, socially, and academically. I'm just really proud of him. I hope you'll stop by to visit me next year when he's in kindergarten," she said.

"For sure. Of course," I replied.

Kindergarten was eighty-seven days away and I had no

idea what C.J.'s next teacher would be like. I hoped that she'd be a lot like Mrs. Meyer or Ms. Kyna, who came before her. I also didn't know what C.J. would be like when he entered kindergarten. There was a time, when we first started seeing Darlene, when I thought the chances were pretty high that he'd socially transition to living as a girl during the summer and enter kindergarten as a female student. He was growing his hair out, giving himself regular manicures and pedicures, wearing clip-on earrings often and lip gloss daily, all while he continued to identify as a boy—albeit one who likes only girl stuff and wants to be treated like a girl.

We were going to be entering elementary school, we were going to be entering more of the unknown, and we were going to be loving our son . . . no matter what.

Conclusion

C.J. ENTERED KINDERGARTEN as a boy, a gender-noncon-forming little boy who has taught us enormous lessons in ex-pectations, empathy, and evolutions.

He's taught us that you don't always get what you expect when you are expecting. You assume that your male child will want to be male, that he'll like traditionally male things, and that he'll be physically and emotionally attracted to women when he grows up. Sometimes that doesn't happen. There is comfort found in expectations, but when they are squashed when your child is three, four, or five years old, you start to question why they exist at all. You attempt to move on with-out expectations and try not to be jaded when people around you hold tight to the old, comfortable ones.

C.J. has taught us that what we want most from other people is empathy. We know that most people do not fully understand the distinctions among gender, sex, and sexuality; we just ask that they have open hearts and open minds and imagine for a minute what our children and we have to deal with on a daily basis. We hope that people will think to them-selves for a moment, *What would I do if I had a child like that?* We would love for people we encounter to learn—as we have—to judge less, imagine more, and treat others as they would like to be treated.

C.J. sparked an evolution in our family when he touched that first Barbie. The evolution was slow, and at times it didn't feel like it was moving forward or it felt as if we were fighting it. But it happened, and no one in our family is the same person they were three years ago. Our multigenerational family has not always gracefully handled the gender nonconformity of its youngest member. For now, we are at different places of acceptance that feel good for everybody, as individuals and as a collective whole. We know where we all stand, even if it's not always side by side.

C.J. has also made us question things.

Have gender-nonconforming kids always existed? Why are they just now being talked about?

Is it okay for a boy to paint his nails and wear a skirt? Where do we draw the line as a society? Is it society's responsibility to draw one at all? Once drawn, can the line be moved? Only forward, but not back?

Are kids who play freely with gender automatically LGBTQ? Would that explain their behavior? Does their behavior need to be explained? Would an explanation make some people feel more comfortable with their behavior? Do they owe anyone—other than themselves—an explanation or feelings of comfortableness?

Is there a benefit to identifying the next generation of the LGBTQ community at a younger age than in generations past? Is it appropriate to think about the sexuality of a child who hasn't even started kindergarten, let alone entered puberty?

I may never have the answers to these questions; I only have opinions that are as fluid as gender and sexuality themselves. What I have offered in these pages is a glimpse into our lives and a hope that people are open and empathetic enough to formulate observations that are respectful of a generation of kids blessed to be able to question gender presentation and sexuality in their childhood without the constraints of outdated social norms.

Hopefully, by raising awareness we'll eventually begin to initiate change and acceptance. I never set out to be an advocate; I just hoped that through my giving people a peek into our lives, their perceptions of LGBTQ kids might start to shift. That they would see that we aren't weird, harmful, or scary; we're just different. If everybody in the world were the same or "normal," this would be a very boring place. People like C.J. give the world color.

And just as we've asked others to be empathetic to us, we've worked as a family to always return the courtesy. We are mindful every day to teach our sons that hate should not breed hate, fear should not breed fear, and prejudice should not breed prejudice. If we lived any other way, the lessons we are teaching our sons would be hypocritical.

Parenting is hard as hell. Matt and I used to stop every once in a while and imagine what life would be like if our boys both conformed to traditional gender norms. It would be so easy to have two boys who acted like boys and were perfectly happy to be boys. When C.J. was younger, there were moments when conformity seemed to reign supreme and we felt life would have been simpler if he weren't so against being a part of the crowd.

Sometimes we spent our days with C.J. so hyperfocused on gender that we wanted to scream out in frustration. There were days when we struggled to leave gender the hell out of everything, days when C.J. asked if the toothpaste, toilet paper, and hand soap he was using were for a girl or for a boy. Now we wouldn't change our experiences and our gender-nonconforming son for anything in the world, and we are disappointed in ourselves because we couldn't always say that.

We are blessed beyond comprehension to have a gender-nonconforming son. It's easy to feel blessed when you get what you expect. But can you feel that way and still be thankful when things turn out not as expected? When things are more different than normal, more challenging than easy? Yes, you can. That is what C.J. taught us.

And what will we teach C.J. and Chase about the blog and this book? In short: everything. They are aware of both already and know that I write about our family and that doing so helps other families with gender-nonconforming kids. I've written every word with them in mind, and I hope that they will hold my words dear to their hearts someday. More than that, I have other cool stuff to show them, like hundreds and hundreds of e-mails of support, letters from people whose lives we've changed, and even notes from parents who gave up struggling with their gender-nonconforming children and started supporting them instead.

My children will know that I was incredibly loving, mindful, and considerate of them in my writing. They'll know that I did all of this for the right reasons.

I've had other people—conservative gossips in particular—question my motives and decisions. They usually ask me what

I'm going to do when people find out that I'm the blogger known as "C.J.'s Mom." They ask me if I'll hide it all from my sons when they get older.

I've always told those people to read my blog and get back to me. Because if you read what I write, I think what you will see above all else is my unconditional love for my children, my support of their unique needs, my struggles as a parent, and my desire for this world to be a more tolerant place.

Notes

Chapter 15

The article I cite from is "Could Your Child Be Gay?" from Parenting.com by Stephanie Dolgoff, found at http://www .parenting.com/article/could-your-child-be-gay? At the end of the chapter, I also briefly cite from "The 'Sissy Boy' Experiment: Why Gender-Related Cases Call for Scientists' Humility," from Time .com, on June, 8, 2011, by Maia Szalavitz, found at http://health land.time.com/2011/06/08/the-sissy-boy-experiment-why-gender-related-cases-call-for-scientists-humility/#ixzz2DvptwwmV.

Chapter 20

The book I reference is *Gender Born, Gender Made,* written by Diane Ehrensaft, PhD, published by the Experiment, 2011.

Chapter 24

When writing about the information I found while researching bullying and LGBTQ youths online, I cite statistics first from the Gay, Lesbian and Straight Education Network's (GLSEN) 2011 National School Climate Survey and then from the 2006 Psychology in the Schools report titled "School Support Groups, Other School Factors, and the Safety of Sexual Minority Adolescents," by Carol Goodenow, Laura Szalacha, and Kim Westheimer. I also consulted the websites of the following organizations: ACLU of Southern California, the Trevor Project, the Seth Walsh Foundation, Human Rights Campaign, It Gets Better, PFLAG, GLSEN, and stopbullying.gov.

When writing about the fraternal birth order effect, I cite from "Boy's Odds of Being Gay Traced to Womb; Study Looks Anew at Puzzling Role of Brothers' Birth Order," from SFGate.com, on June 27, 2006, by Sabin Russell, found at: http://www.sfgate.com/news/article/Boy-s-odds-of-being-gay-traced-to-womb-Study-2494005.php.

Chapter 35

I cited from the "Seth Walsh Students' Rights Project" and "LGBTQ Students, Know Your Rights: You Have the Right to Be Yourself" handouts provided by the American Civil Liberties Union of Southern California (ACLU-SC) at www.aclu-sc.org, and a public letter about bullying and the Title IX of the Education Amendments of 1972, dated October 26, 2010, written by Russlynn Ali, assistant secretary for civil rights, United States Department of Education.

Acknowledgments

Thank you to Matt, my co-adventurer and world's greatest partner, for letting me be me and for letting me check out of our lives to write when necessary. Your infinite amount of support, patience, kindness, and love astounds me. I'm beyond lucky to have you, love you, and be loved by you every minute of forever.

Thank you to Alison Schwartz (formerly of ICM) for finding me, holding my hand through the process of selling a book, and when it was time to chase your dream, for passing me to the awesome Kari Stuart at ICM. Thank you, Kari, for being a friend, advocate, confidante, and supporter and for always believing in me and the potential of this book.

Thank you to Jenna Ciongoli and Crown/Random House for seeing the need for this book and trusting me to write it. Thank you for wanting it to succeed almost as much as I do and for constantly wanting me to dig deeper, be more sincere, genuine, and poignant to the point that I didn't know if I could be any more of those things. In a way you were a free therapist for the better part of six months.

Thank you to Domenica Alioto for taking me under your wing when sweet baby Gus made his appearance.

Thanks to my brother for living the life he did and letting me learn from it. And for being a source of constant support, advice, laughter, education, love, and honesty. I've loved you for as long as I can remember and know that won't change . . . ever.

Thank you to my parents for this life I have and for allowing me to write about it. Thank you for your honesty and support as I wrote, the tears we shed alone and together, and for everything you do for our family. You are appreciated and loved. Thank you for making me the woman and mother I am today and for loving your grandkids endlessly.

Thank you to L&L for providing a place for me to write, letting me stay in my pajamas all day, for cooking my meals, mixing my drinks, doing my puzzles, and listening to my music. Thank you for loving me like a daughter, raising a good man for me to love, and being great grandparents.

Thank you to my BFF, KK. (KK, this is me standing up and receiving an Oscar and thanking other people ahead of you but really thanking you first.) Thank you, pea, for being another source of powerful unconditional love in my life and the lives of my boys. I'll meet you in Laguna. You bring the cats and boxed wine.

Thank you to my group of amazing friends who have, more often than not, heard me use "the book" as an excuse for forgetting birthdays, canceling get-togethers, and not returning phone calls. We need to make up for lost time and the first round is on me. Nicki, I owe you especially.

Thank you to everyone who agreed to be interviewed, participate, and/or be mentioned in this book. If your name is in this book, I thank you for positively affecting my family's life. (If I wrote negatively about you and you wish that I had written nicer words, then you probably should have behaved better.)

Thank you to Darlene for changing the way we parent and for being a part of our team. Thank you to Lisa for allowing me to keep my day job while pursuing my passion.

Thank you to Neil and David for being so welcoming to my family. Thank you for writing the foreword to this book and offering your support. I owe you; I just don't know how I'll ever manage to repay you.

Last, but in no way least, thank you to my blog's loyal and engaged readers. Without you I would not have a blog, a book, confidence, or hope. You all have changed my life.

Cheers,
Lori

ABOUT THE AUTHOR

Lori Duron is a public relations consultant, blogger, and writer. She earned a bachelor's degree in English with an emphasis in literature and a minor in communications from a Lutheran university that may not approve of the content of this book. Her blog about the adventures in raising a fabulous, gender-creative son has more than one million readers in nearly 180 countries, including gender studies students and faculty at more than fifty colleges and universities in the United States, Canada, and the UK.

She has been named one of BlogHer's "2011 Voices of the Year," one of Ignite Social Media's "100 Women Bloggers You Should Be Reading," one of Circle of Moms' "Top 25 SoCal Moms," and one of *Parents* magazine's top three blogs "Most Likely to Inspire You to Change the World." She also won best dressed in high school.

She lives with her husband and two children in a happy, messy home in Orange County, California.

www.RaisingMyRainbow.com
Facebook.com/RaisingMyRainbow
Twitter.com/RaisingRainbow

Raising My Rainbow

A Reader's Guide for
Raising My Rainbow

1. When did you first learn the distinct differences between sex, gender, and sexuality? What prompted you to need to know the differences?

2. Do you believe that a child's gender expression and sexuality are more nature or nurture?

3. Why is effeminacy in males so often deemed a weakness? Why is masculinity in females so often seen as a strength?

4. If you had a daughter, would you allow her to wear a sports jersey to school? If you had a son, would you allow him to wear a dress to school? Why or why not? If your answers differ, why is there a double standard?

5. Can you parent to the best of your ability when you are concerned about what other people will think or say?

6. What role does community/society play in how we raise our children and our want for them to conform? Why do we want them to conform? So that other people won't talk/think/judge? To save them

from harassment and bullying? Is forcing a child to conform really protecting him or her?

7. If your child is going to be LGBTQ, would you want to know when he or she is three? Six? Ten? Thirteen? Sixteen? Twenty? Twenty-three? When is the "right age"?

8. Do you think it is possible for an LGBTQ child to never have to "come out," to be just as open about being gay as most kids are about being straight?

9. If someone said that when your children are in the room you should always conduct yourself as if an LGBTQ person is in the room to be safe because you never know your children's future sexuality or gender, how would that make you feel?

10. If someone you knew had a child who was LGBTQ, would you feel bad for them? Happy for them? Jealous of them? Why?

11. Are you teaching your child about empathy just as much as you teach him or her other life lessons and skills? If your child saw a boy wearing a skirt out in public, what would he or she say? Is there anything that you can do now to prepare them for something like this?

12. How would members of your family react if your child was LGBTQ? Are there some members who would be better about it than others? What would you do if there were members of your family who were not supportive of your child?

13. What role do you think religion plays in society's enforcement of gender and sexuality norms?

14. If during a routine ultrasound it could be discovered that a baby was LGBTQ, do you think parents

would want to know? What would be the benefits of knowing? What would be the drawbacks? How could parents react wonderfully to knowing? How could parents react horribly?

15. On the gender spectrum of masculine all the way to the left and feminine all the way to the right, where do you think you fall? Is it the same every day? Every week? Every month? Every year? Have you ever played with gender presentation? How did it feel?

Twelve Things Every Gender-Nonconforming Child Wants You to Know

1. When most people are born, their sex (male or female based on their genitalia) and their gender (male or female based on their brain) are usually in total alignment. Mine aren't. Get over it. I was born this way.

2. If you are confused and can't quite tell if I'm a boy or a girl, just know that I am a person. Please treat me that way.

3. Sometimes I notice that my gender nonconformity makes you uncomfortable. I'm not trying to make you uncomfortable; I'm trying to make myself comfortable.

4. My gender nonconformity is a way of expressing myself, a way of being true to myself, true to the way my heart beats and my blood flows. I allow you to express your gender your way without being bothered; I hope that you will allow me to do the same.

5. It's silly when you think, say, or feel that colors, clothes, and/or toys are "only for girls" or "only for boys." Colors, toys, and clothes are for

everybody—even though one particular item may be marketed only to one sex or gender. Antiquated notions like "dolls are only for girls" have no reason to exist, and I see them as pure nonsense.

6. Just because I'm gender nonconforming doesn't mean that I'll grow up to be LGBTQ. It's a strong predictor, but I'd rather you see me as a child and not an underage punch line to some homophobic joke.

7. It hurts my feelings when people point and laugh at me because of my gender nonconformity. I'm not weird; I'm just different. I don't need people pointing out my differences—especially people who are old enough to know better.

8. I don't ask that you teach everyone around me about sex, gender, and sexuality, but if you could teach them about empathy, kindness, and acceptance, I would greatly appreciate it. Treat others how you want to be treated—it's that simple.

9. I don't fit into a category or a box. I may not be easy to explain or understand, but if you approach me with an open heart and an open mind, I can guarantee that I will change your way of thinking. It makes me sad when I learn that your mind and heart are closed.

10. Kids like me are the most likely to suffer from depression, addiction, and bullying; practice unsafe sex; and injure ourselves or die by self-harm. Please refrain from making me hate myself because I am different. My gender nonconformity should not be a thing of shame.

11. Bullies aren't just at school; sometimes they are at

home too. Home should be the place where I feel the most safe and the most loved. If that is not the case, something is wrong and I need help.

12. If you see me doing something that defies "traditional gender norms," don't place blame on my parents or family. Give them praise! It means that they are awesome enough to understand that I need their love and support more than anything. Them forcing me to express a gender that I don't exactly associate with or trying to "fix" me would do dangerous things to me. I don't need them to tell me to "act like a lady" or "man up." I need them to tell me that I was perfectly created. If everybody in the world were the same or "expected" to be the same, this would be a very boring world. People like me give the world color.

Tips for Educators

No matter the age or grade level, if you have a career in education, you will teach lesbian, gay, bisexual, transgender, and questioning (LGBTQ) and gender-nonconforming children.

More than 3 percent of the population identifies as LGBTQ. That means that if there are thirty students in a class, at least one of them is LGBTQ. And, gender variance or a transgender identity occurs in as many as one of every five hundred births—making it more common than childhood diabetes.

Educators have the unique opportunity to change stereotypes, address social injustices, decrease bullying, and increase empathy and acceptance. Please plan your curriculum and classroom accordingly. Consider implementing these tips in an age-appropriate manner:

1. Emphasize that the members of the class are a community and every child is needed, special, unique, valued, and has something different to offer the community. If everybody were exactly the same, the community would be boring.

2. Ensure that every child in the classroom feels safe and included. Let children know that they should be working to make others feel safe and included, as well. It's not just the teacher's job; it's everybody's job.

3. Teach children about empathy. Educators don't have to provide in-depth lessons on gender, sex, and sexuality, but they do have a responsibility to teach children about empathy, kindness, and acceptance. Children need to be taught how to work, play, and get along with all kinds of people.

4. Create an inclusive and accepting environment that teaches children to recognize and resist stereotypes. Introduce them to books that show children and adults in atypical gender roles and use gender neutral terms when discussing careers and members of the community (i.e., police officer instead of policeman).

5. Explain to children that everyone has their own style and that people are allowed to dress and wear their hair any way they want. Everyone gets to pick their own style. If you like someone's style, tell them. Compliments should be shared, criticisms should not.

6. Make your classroom a place where all children are free to learn and play without the strict confines of stereotypes. All colors, games, activities, and toys can be enjoyed by everyone. Nothing is "just for boys" or "just for girls."

7. Resist the urge to use gender to divide students into lines, groups, or teams. That makes some students feel uncomfortable and distracts them. It's

hard to teach a child when she or he is distracted or uncomfortable. Try something new.

8. Eliminate gender when addressing pupils. Instead, address them using gender-neutral terms, like students, friends, scholars, class, children, people, human beings, etc.

9. Know the nation's and your state's anti-bullying and anti-discrimination laws. Teach students about the laws and how to stand up for themselves and others, to resist bullying, and to work together. Empower children to be allies.

10. View parents of LGBTQ and gender-nonconforming children as resources and teammates, not high-maintenance liabilities. It's not two teams against each other; it's one team in favor of the child. Also realize that sometimes bullies aren't just at school; sometimes they are at home. If you see a child in distress, help him or her.

Resources

ACLU
Working daily in courts, legislatures, and communities to defend and preserve the individual rights and liberties that the Constitution and laws of the United States guarantee everyone.

www.aclu.org
Facebook.com/aclu.nationwide
Twitter.com/aclu

Children's National Medical Center's Gender and Sexuality Psychosocial Programs
Offers a parent guide, an outreach program, a local support group, a national Listserv, a summer camp, and an outpatient clinical program.

www.childrensnational.org/gendervariance

Gender Odyssey
Interested in the thoughtful exploration of gender and provides an environment where people of all genders can share their experiences and learn from the experiences of others.

www.genderodyssey.org
Facebook.com/genderodyssey
Twitter.com/genderodyssey

Gender Spectrum

Provides education, training, and support to help create a gender sensitive and inclusive environment for all children and teens.

www.genderspectrum.org
Facebook.com/genderspectrum
Twitter.com/genderspectrum

GLAAD

Amplifying the voice of the LGBT community by empowering real people to share their stories, holding the media accountable for the words and images they present, and helping grassroots organizations communicate effectively.

www.glaad.org
Facebook.com/glaad
Twitter.com/glaad

GLSEN

Leading national education organization focused on ensuring safe schools for all students.

www.glsen.org
Facebook.com/glsen
Twitter.com/glsen

Human Rights Campaign

Working for lesbian, gay, bisexual, and transgender equal rights.

www.hrc.org
Facebook.com/humanrightscampaign
Twitter.com/hrc

It Gets Better

Communicating to lesbian, gay, bisexual, and transgender youth around the world that it gets better.

www.itgetsbetter.org
Facebook.com/itgetsbetterproject
Twitter.com/itgetsbetter

Lambda Legal (Bending the Mold Toolkit)

Oldest and largest national legal organization whose mission is to achieve full recognition of the civil rights of lesbians, gay men, bisexuals, transgender people, and those with HIV through impact litigation, education, and public policy work.

www.lambdalegal.org
Facebook.com/lambdalegal
Twitter.com/lambdalegal

Matthew Shepard Foundation

Persuading people to think differently, behave differently, and inform others of the importance and value of diversity.

www.matthewshepard.org
Facebook.com/matthew.shepard.foundation
Twitter.com/mattshepardfdn

PFLAG

The nation's largest organization for parents, families, friends, and allies united with LGBTQ people to move forward through support, education, and advocacy.

    www.pflag.org

    Facebook.com/PFLAG

    Twitter.com/PFLAG

Teaching Tolerance

Promotes an appreciation for diversity in schools by reducing prejudice, improving intergroup relations, and supporting equity for our nation's children. Provides free educational materials to teachers and other school practitioners.

    www.tolerance.org

    Facebook.com/teachingtolerance.org

    Twitter.com/tolerance_org

The Trevor Project

Providing crisis intervention and suicide prevention services to lesbian, gay, bisexual, transgender, and questioning youth. If you are a youth who is feeling alone, confused, or in crisis, please call the Trevor Lifeline at 1-866-488-7386 for immediate help.

    www.thetrevorproject.org

    Facebook.com/thetrevorproject

    Twitter.com/trevorproject

Welcoming Schools

Offers tools, lessons, and resources on embracing family diversity, avoiding gender stereotyping, and ending bullying and name-calling in elementary schools.

www.welcomingschools.org
Facebook.com/welcomingschools

WPATH
Devoted to the understanding and treatment of gender
identity disorders.
www.wpath.org
Twitter.com/wpath

If you are in crisis or in need of immediate support
please call:

The National Suicide Prevention Lifeline
1-800-273-TALK (8255)

The Trevor Project
1-866-4-U-TREVOR (866-488-7386)

The GLBT National Help Center Hotline
1-888-THE-GLNH (888-843-4564)

The GLBT National Youth Talkline
1-800-246-PRIDE (800-246-7743)